MASTER
PUBLIC
SPEAKING

Anne Nicholls
Third Edition

'We're just not impressed by your body language!'

How To Books

Dedication

This book is dedicated first to my father, Kenneth Hulbert, who despite having a severe stammer throughout life is a great communicator and lover of the English language; and second to my mother, Elizabeth Hulbert, who helped him through on many occasions when he was lost for words.

First edition 1991
Second edition 1993
Third edition 1995

British Library Cataloguing in Publication Data
A catalogue record for this book is available from the British Library.

© Copyright 1991, 1993 and 1995 by Anne Nicholls.
Published by How To Books Ltd, Plymbridge House, Estover Road, Plymouth PL6 7PZ, United Kingdom. Tel: (01752) 735251/695745. Fax: (01752) 695699. Telex: 45635.

Note: The material contained in this book is set out in good faith for general guidance and no liability can be accepted for loss or expense incurred as a result of relying in particular circumstances on statements made in the book. The laws and regulations are complex and liable to change, and readers should check the current position with the relevant authorities before making personal arrangements.

Typeset by PDQ Typesetting, Stoke-on-Trent.
Printed and bound by The Cromwell Press, Broughton Gifford, Melksham, Wiltshire.

Contents

Preface

to the Third Edition

Ask a group of ten people, selected at random, the question: 'What is the one thing that frightens you more than anything else?' and you can bet that at least four will say: 'Speaking in public'.

An American survey some years ago found that some people were more afraid of public speaking than nuclear war, death and financial ruin. What is the key to explaining this irrational fear? Perhaps it is that we suddenly feel very exposed, which is very unnerving. It's rather like having your outer protective shell peeled off—there is nothing left to hide behind. It's far worse than stage fright because it's the *real* you out there, not just an actor playing a part.

It's surprising how many captains of industry and people at the top of their profession flounder when it comes to giving public presentations. Have you ever been to a conference or attended a lecture given by a 'big name' and found yourself being totally bored because the speaker fails to communicate?

So what makes one person totally absorbing and another excruciatingly boring? The answer is not a simple one. There is no one simple formula for learning the skills of speaking in public or delivering a paper in an interesting way. Some people seem to be able to do it effortlessly, others struggle. However, there are techniques which everyone can learn, and some common pitfalls to avoid.

Understanding the psychology of your audience is the first step. If you don't understand what it is they want to hear you are wasting your time. (Chapter 3). Meticulous preparation and structuring is vital (Chapter 4). Then there is the question of how to put it across. Some people, such as the botanist David Bellamy, have a gift for making a boring subject riveting. This book will give you exercises to practise your vocal skills (Chapter 6). The visual aspect of communication—eye contact, body language, visual aids—is equally important (Chapters 7 and 8). Then there are techniques for overcoming nerves using breathing and visualisation (Chapter 9). And finally, you will be getting tips on what to do on the day, how to think on your feet, and how to react if you are invited to appear on radio or television.

This book will cover both *what* you say, and *how* you say it. At school we are taught to read, write, add up figures, find rivers on maps, learn dates and argue points logically in writing. However, somehow it is assumed that we can all speak and communicate and that we don't need to be taught how to do it. The gift of the gab is believed to be something you've got or you haven't—like style.

It is true that some people are born with silver tongues. The Welsh for instance have a long tradition of being great orators. Anyone who wants to make a career in politics or public life has simply got to learn how to speak well in public—and learn is just what they do. Consider the deaf Labour MP Jack Ashley. He suffers from one of the most severe handicaps in a profession where speaking with fluency and conviction is all-important: he cannot even hear his own voice. Yet he has overcome this huge obstacle and made a success of a career in politics by capitalising on it and becoming the champion of the disabled.

Another success story is the percussionist Evelyn Glennie—deaf from the age of 11. She appears on television introducing orchestral works and percussion pieces to audiences of millions, yet no-one would ever know that she cannot hear her own voice yet alone the noise of the percussion instruments she plays.

If people with that degree of disability can become successful communicators then you should have no difficulty at all. Even the great actor Laurence Olivier suffered from terrible stage fright for years and many confident speakers admit to having nerves before meeting an audience—they just have ways of dealing with them and psyching themselves up.

The assumption, therefore, in this book is that *anyone* can become a competent public speaker or communicator, given the motivation and the ability to learn some basic techniques. Simply reading this book, however, will not make you a good speaker. You need to practise the vocal exercises, gain experience with different audiences, take risks on occasions and, above all, learn from your mistakes.

Anne Nicholls

1
What Skills do You Need to be a Good Speaker?

When did you last hear a speaker so riveting that you sat spellbound, unable to let your concentration wander for one second? Was it a teacher at school, or a university lecturer? Perhaps someone you heard at a seminar, public meeting or in church? Or possibly you have a favourite television personality who can make the dullest subject totally absorbing. (Have you heard the botanist David Bellamy enthusing about peat bogs?)

All great communicators have one thing in common—they understand what **motivates an audience to listen**. Understanding motivation is fundamental to anyone who is going to make a success as a communicator. You don't give the audience what you want them to hear—you given them what they *need*. That doesn't mean to say that you have to start swotting up on psychology. Many brilliant communicators have an instinctive understanding of how people tick and how to give them what they want. Just walk down Petticoat Lane or Berwick Street market in London and listen to the costermongers.

Think of your favourite speakers again and analyse what made them so special. Was it *what* they said, *how* they said it, how they *sounded* or how they *looked*? Try and remember as much as you can about the content. Can you remember the salient points, or was it some anecdote or incident that sticks in your mind?

Some of the greatest communicators are (or were) politicians or academics-turned-media presenters. Three come to mind. The archaeologist and historian John Romer, who has presented TV series on Ancient Egyptian Civilization and Biblical History; the scientist and presenter of the *Ascent of Man*, the late Dr Jacob Bronowski; and the botanist David Bellamy. All three are scholars but they also possess 'the common touch'. None speak or spoke the Queen's English—John Romer has distinct Cockney vowels, David Bellamy seems to slobber as he speaks and Dr Bronowski had a thick Eastern European accent and an irritating habit of shaping his hand like an upturned bunch of bananas. The qualities that each one has (or had) in abundance were a love of the subject and the ability to make a remote, academic subject somehow relevant to ordinary people. John Romer for example talks about ancient Egyptians as if they were ordinary people doing their weekly shopping.

Now try and recall the most *boring* speaker or teacher you have ever heard. What was it that made you switch off? Was it a nervous twitch that stopped you concentrating on what they were saying, or the persistent drone of their voice? Perhaps the subject matter could have been interesting but the speaker simply lacked enthusiasm. Or maybe they were so wrapped up in their subject that they failed to consider the most important factor—the audience. Take ancient history, for example. This can be the most deadly dull subject if the speaker or teacher cannot make it relevant to the needs and interests of ordinary people.

- The central theme of this book is the **needs of the audience.**

Before you even start thinking about what you are going to say and how you are going to deliver it you need to understand how people listen and what makes them *want* to listen. It's very basic psychology.

In this chapter we will explore what makes a good speaker and see which of these skills can be learned.

TRUTHS AND FALLACIES

First of all, let's look at some of the things people have said about public speaking and oratory.

- You must have perfect diction to be a good speaker.

Wrong. Many great and popular speakers have a speech impediment. Former Prime Minister Winston Churchill had. TV personalities Frank Muir and Jonathan Ross have trouble with their 'R's' yet both are in constant demand as after-dinner speakers. Janet Street-Porter of the screeching vocals and rasping vowels certainly makes you sit up and listen. The Queen has a beautiful speaking voice but she is not a very relaxed speaker, unlike her eldest son.

- Good speakers are born, not made.

Wrong. Some people may have more of a natural aptitude, but most trainers in public speaking—such as Greville Janner MP, who trains business executives and politicians in presentation skills and media handling—insist that *anyone* can be taught to be a competent speaker.

Humphrey Walters, Managing Director of the international skills training organisation MaST (Management and Skills Training), an accomplished and highly relaxed speaker himself, firmly believes that becoming a good speaker is simply a matter of practice. The secret is thorough preparation. 'Failing to prepare is preparing to fail,' he says.

- Good speakers don't need to know a lot about their subject—they can be taught to deliver a speech like an actor speaking lines.

Right and wrong. Professional broadcasters have the knack of reading from a script whilst managing to sound as if they really know a lot about the subject. On the other hand, to be really convincing, you need to have enthusiasm or even passion about a subject. Having a strong personality helps. Ludovic Kennedy, in his BBC TV series *A Gift of the Gab*, says that there are two qualities that make us sit up and listen. The first is the speaker's own personality—the innate attraction that emanates from him (or her), and secondly, the acquisition of some simple rules which most natural speakers pick up unconsciously. (These will be discussed in Chapters 5 and 7).

- Being able to speak fluently is something that comes from the heart. If you try and learn 'tricks of the trade' or concentrate on techniques and structure, then it will impede the flow of words.

Mostly wrong. There are some very useful hints (which is what this book is all about) which will help you to turn an amateurish presentation into a professional one. Some of the techniques, many of which have been known for centuries, which will be discussed are

- the rhetorical question with the punchy reply;
- the rule of threes;
- using repetition and rhythm to emphasise a point;
- use of simple, direct language designed to be *spoken*, not read;
- short sentences (with the occasional long one);
- use of pauses and timing;
- the ability to include variety into the vocal tone;
- making eye contact with the audience; and
- maintaining a relaxed body posture.

Gladstone, for instance, had six rules for speaking (some of which have already been mentioned); use simple words, short sentences, distinct diction, test your arguments beforehand, know your subject, and watch the audience. (Bear in mind that, whilst these simple rules have stood the test of time, Gladstone's oratory today would sound pompous, verbose and long-winded.) According to eye-witnesses,

Gladstone had a fine voice with great depth and variety of tone, a keen eye and the ability to use sweeping gestures without looking unnatural.

- It ain't what you say, it's the way that you say it.

Right and wrong. The Greek orator Demosthenes, when asked what were the three requisites for oratory, replied: 'Delivery, delivery and delivery'. A bad speaker can make a superb speech yet send an audience off to sleep within two minutes by mumbling his way through it. One of the problems with running conferences is that, whilst there may be some speakers who have something wholly original and spell-binding to say, if they don't have the skills to hold an audience the whole thing will fall flat. On the other hand, there are speakers who talk garbage and still manage to hold the audience simply by the sound of their voice and physical presence. Americans can be particularly good at it. Read the 'I have a dream speech' by Martin Luther King in Chapter 5. It is all words with little tangible content and therefore should be spoken not read, but it is cited as being a great speech because it encapsulated the wishes and desires of American blacks at that time. People who have heard Jessie Jackson speak say that he has the ability to leave his audience in a state of euphoria vowing to vote him in as President. Apparently, it has little to do with rational argument although what he says *seems* to make sense in a very basic way.

A point worth making here is that great public speeches are often low on reason and high on emotion. Few of Hitler's speeches contained any rational argument but he had the ability to whip up his audience into such a state of frenzy that they would believe blatant lies.

In this book we will look at the different skills you need to master to become a fluent speaker and deliver professional presentations. No-one expects you to drive audiences into a frenzy or reproduce the magic of Laurence Olivier. What we *do* intend is to turn you into a competent and relaxed speaker so that you can survive on your feet. Obviously, simply reading this book won't make you a good speaker—you will need to practise the exercises and put yourself in front of an audience. However, there are some useful tips which will make the difference between an amateur and professional presentation—simple hints on body language, use of audio-visual aids and ways of dealing with nerves, for instance. A great deal of attention will be paid to understanding the *audience* and their needs—what makes

them listen and what makes them switch off. And you will have lots of
checklists to help you do your preparation thoroughly.

WHAT MAKES A GOOD COMMUNICATOR?

Cicero (Roman philosopher/writer)
'In an orator we must demand the thoughts of a philosopher, the
subtlety of the magician, a diction almost poetic, a lawyer's memory,
the voice of a tragedian and the consummate bearing of an actor.'
(Translated from Latin).

Demosthenes (Greek philosopher/writer)
'Delivery, delivery and delivery'.

Quintilian (Roman orator)
His advice to orators was to be clear, brief and credible. 'Language of
but moderate quality, if recommended by forcible delivery, will
produce a more powerful effect than the most excellent language, if
deprived of that advantage.'

Ludovic Kennedy (TV journalist/presenter)
The three most important qualities in a good speaker are '...a relaxed
stance, the careful use of gesture and short simple sentences.'

Harold Macmillan (Prime Minister, 1957-63)
Commenting on the advice given to him by David Lloyd George
before his maiden speech in the House of Commons: 'Vary the pitch
and vary the pace and remember the most vital thing in a speech, if
you can do it, is the pause... Never make a gesture from the elbow—
that's a very weak gesture ... If you can make it at all it must come
from the shoulder... and the other great thing is the gesture must
precede the phrase.'

Greville Janner MP (Chairman of *Effective Presentation Skills*)
'The greatest magic is the pause.'

WHAT SKILLS DO YOU NEED TO BE A GOOD SPEAKER?

In this book you will learn the following key skills of self-presentation:

1. How to understand the needs of the audience.

2. How to write and structure material in a way that makes it easy
   to follow.

3. How to choose words and phrases which give a subject life and depth.

4. How to prepare and research material thoroughly.

5. How to rehearse and prepare yourself.

6. How to appreciate the difference between written and spoken English and how to write speech.

7. How to achieve variety and flexibility. Your voice should be capable of changing pitch, speed, volume and tone.

8. How to use pauses effectively.

9. How to have a relaxed posture and body movement.

10. How to maintain eye contact with the audience.

11. How to present yourself visually to suit particular audiences.

12. How to use audio-visual aids correctly.

13. How to get rid of nerves: some simple techniques.

14. How to develop your self-confidence.

2
Deciding Your
Purpose and Message

Too many speakers fail because of muddled thinking. They don't really know *what* they are trying to communicate or *why*. They may have been told to prepare a short presentation by someone else, who hasn't thought out the purpose of the exercise either. The solution?— to sit down and think through the rationale and then write clear objectives.

A hypothetical situation

You've been asked to give a talk on the history of Tibetan widgets at your local library because you happen to be an expert on the subject and known in the local community. You have no idea who the audience will be but the librarian assures you there will *be* an audience made up of members of the local history and antiques society.

Now ask yourself the following questions:

- Why should I want to talk about Tibetan widgets?
- Why should anybody want to listen to me?
- What single message would I want to put across?
- When I have finished speaking what need in the audience do I want to have satisfied?
- When they all walk away what state would I like them to leave in?

This may seem very basic stuff, but it's amazing how often speakers will launch into their pet subject with great enthusiasm without pausing to consider what their purpose is and whether the audience share the same enthusiasm. They ignore the *needs* of the audience.

Take a lesson from the world of advertising. Successful advertisers can turn anything from monkey nuts and rubber washers into objects of great fascination by using some very basic techniques; they can make millions of people believe that they really *need* monkey nuts and rubber washers in their lives. They set out with a clear purpose—for example to increase sales of rubber washers to single males between the ages of 25 and 45 living in the south-east—and they know what technique they are going to use to persuade the target group that their life will be impossible without them.

Chapter 3 will discuss the importance of understanding the needs of the audiences in more detail.

A useful exercise is to break down communication into certain components and stages by using *communication models*. This book is essentially a practical guide, but you might find this little bit of theory helpful.

COMMUNICATION MODELS

The purpose of looking at communication models is that they help people to clarify the message, the audience it is aimed at, the choice of medium and method (speech, writing, etc) and the reason for communicating.

A communications theorist called Lasswell gave a useful definition of communication:

- 'Who says what in what channel to whom with what effect'.

Breaking this down further we have the following components in the process of communication.

The sender (Encoder)   the person sending the message (who).

The receiver (Decoder)   The person (or people) receiving the message (whom).

The Message   The content or main purpose (what).

The code   The 'language' in which the message is sent. We talk about Morse code as a *code* because we don't understand it. Language is also a code. So are images and musical sounds. So the SENDER and RECEIVER of communication are ENCODERS and DECODERS because they translate thoughts into coded form.

The channel   The medium you choose for communicating the message or *how* you send the message—by writing on paper, through speech, music, moving images, still pictures, or digital signals, for instance.

When you are preparing a speech, think whether speech is the best or the only way of getting across your message.

'Noise'   This means any interference in the channel of communication from crackling on the telephone line to a thunderstorm outside. In communication theory it is extended to cover anything which interferes with the communication of a message from sender to receiver. So 'noise' can include for example the speaker's irritating mannerisms, poor visuals, not being able to hear at the back, using jargon that people don't understand, and so on.

EXERCISE

For each of the following situations below you have a **sender** (yourself) and a **receiver** (stated). Now choose the most appropriate **channel**, selecting from the list. For instance, semaphore is hardly the best way of conveying intense emotions, nor is Morse code the best way of writing poetry! In some cases, more than one form of communication is necessary. (Suggested answers on p. 41.)

1.   News of redundancies to a workforce of about 1,000.

2.   Launch of a new product on the market to an audience of press and retailers.

3.   Condolences to a friend on losing their spouse.

4.   Instructions to a group of novices on how to sail a boat. (Assume it's their first lesson.)

5.   The life and work of Vincent Van Gogh to an audience at the local arts society.

6.   Explaining a new office telecommunications system to office staff (about 40).

7.   Health and Safety procedures to staff (about 100).

8.   Explaining the National Curriculum to teachers.

9.   Notice of an emergency meeting at 24 hours' notice.

10.   Instructions to isolated platoons in a desert land army.

Some methods or channels of communication

Speech (in face-to-face situations)
Music
A letter
A newspaper story
A telegram
A notice
An advertisement in a magazine or newspaper
A TV news bulletin
Colour transparencies (projected onto a screen)
Words or graphics on an overhead projector
Touch
Semaphore
Morse code
Burning beacons
An announcement on the radio or news story
A telephone conversation
A painting
Fax
Sound over a loudspeaker

CLARIFYING YOUR PURPOSE

Lord Reith, founder of the BBC, always said that the three main purposes of broadcast radio were to

> educate
> inform
> entertain

To this trio add   persuade

Too often, speakers ramble on with no clear idea of what they are trying to say and why the audience has assembled in the first place. Take a typical amateur soap-box orator at Speaker's Corner in London, ranting on the coming of the revolution/end of the world/ global holocaust. Nobody takes such people seriously because they haven't stopped to think about their message and who they are trying to persuade. You may feel passionate about political freedom in Ruritania but your audience won't care less it they don't feel it's relevant to them and you haven't clarified your message for them.

Stop for a moment and start to clarify the purpose of your communication. Just 'to help people understand the plight of peasants in Ruritania' is not specific enough. Nor does it necessarily relate to the needs of the audience, or meet any immediate needs.

Take a subject closer to home—education and training. Enough has been written and said about Britain's appalling track record in training compared to countries like Germany and the USA, but try convincing a small or medium sized company that they need to invest in training during a recession and they will throw up their hands in horror saying they can't afford it. One of the first things to be cut in hard times is the training budget. However, if you show how training can solve any of their immediate problems like staff recruitment, poor motivation, plummeting sales, and point out **benefits** in terms of the bottom line (ie money) then your audience is more likely to listen to what you have to say.

DECIDING ON YOUR MESSAGE AND SETTING CLEAR OBJECTIVES

The most important part of your preparation

Unless you want people to fidget, fall asleep or walk out, you *must* have something to say that your audience will *want* to hear.

Let's suppose that you have been asked to give a talk to 16-year-olds about career choice. There are lots of things you can talk about—where to go to get advice, what the local careers service can offer, the mistakes that people make when choosing a career, how not to follow blindly in your parents' footsteps and so on. Of all these messages, there must be one which is paramount. Let's assume that it is: *To tell them about the local Careers Office.* Does this sound a little vague? It needs to be sharpened up. How about: *To tell them how the local Careers Office can help them decide about their future career and choose the best subjects to study.* Better.

In *How to Give a Successful Presentation* the author, training consultant Ian Richards, says that the essence of a good message is that 'it will trigger an emotional response' in the audience. You need to find out what they really care about and what their needs are. **You need to sell benefits not features.**

Take your message again. *To tell them how the local Careers Office can help them decide about their future career and choose the best subjects to study.* What changes would you like to make in your audiences of 16-year-olds? Let's say you want them to go and make an appointment to see the Careers Office after they have listened to you, so you will need to inspire them as well as inform them.

Let's start to refine your message and break it up into small sections.

At the end of this speech, the audience should know

- Where the Careers Office is situated.
- What kind of information and resources are available.
- What happens at a careers interview.
- How they would individually benefit from a visit.

The last point can be broken down even further.

- How they would benefit from a visit. They would:
  - discover their main skills and aptitudes;
  - find out about different careers they might want to pursue;
  - learn about courses available;
  - spend a fun hour doing computer tests;
  - get away from school for a morning.

The last two points could well be the strongest selling points for that audience. If they think it will be fun they might well *want* to make a visit—not because they think they *ought* to. Consider how the objectives would differ for an adult who has recently lost his or her job and was visiting the Careers Office to seek help and guidance in getting another job. Spending a morning doing 'fun exercises' and nothing else will leave such a person feeling pretty dissatisfied.

The main point about setting clear objectives is that they should be **quantifiable**, otherwise you won't know if the objectives have been met and your message has got across.

A *goal* or *aim* may be fairly general, but an *objective* must be more specific. An aim is something fairly broad such as 'To tell International Widgets plc about the benefits of training', but an objective needs to be measurable and (preferably) quantifiable as well. In other words, you need to focus.

Take your general aim of telling International Widgets plc about training and focus it down in stages, and we get:

- To show the benefits of training in terms of solving problems in the company.
- To show the benefits of training in terms of solving
  (a) problems of recruitment
  (b) problems of staff motivation

(c) problems of falling sales
(d) problems of dwindling profits

- To show the benefits of training in the three areas mentioned with the single purpose of selling a distance learning pack on *Managing Your Business*.

- To sell one pack of *Managing Your Business*.

The message here is that you need to get inside the head of the receiver of your communication and have empathy with their needs. People won't buy a product or an ideal simply because someone tells them they ought to. One of the worst mistakes a speaker can make is to start with something like: 'I am going to convince you that...'. The audience will switch off. The other mistake is to assume the message they are putting across is identical to the one the audience thinks it is receiving.

- Remember: 'The meaning of a communication is the *response* it gets (Bandler and Grinder). Think about it!

EXERCISE

Here are five different subjects on which you have been asked to prepare a lecture, presentation, talk or speech, together with the audience. In one sentence, write down the main point or core statement that you would want to get across in **less than 10 words**.

Example

Subject	Your first week at university.
Audience	New students ('freshers').
Core statement	To reassure freshers that they are entering a caring community.

Subject	*Audience/Situation*
1. The National Curriculum. *Core statement:*	Parents/PTA meeting. _____ _____
2. Nineteenth-century English watercolours. *Core statement:*	Art collectors/Lecture at Christies _____ _____

3. Desk-Top Publishing (DTP).   Graphic design studio/
                                    Sales presentation from
                                    DTP supplier.

    Core statement: _____

                                   _____

4. Cricket.   Local cricket club/Annual
                                    dinner.

    Core statement: _____

                                   _____

5. Leadership.   Senior managers in a
                                    manufacturing company/
                                    Training seminar

    Core statement: _____

                                   _____

6. Add your own pet subject here.
    Core statement: _____

                                   _____

CHECKLIST

- Can you put down in one short sentence (less than 10 words) the single main message you want to communicate?

- Is your message *quantifiable*—how do you intend to measure whether the audience has received your message and learned from it?

- Can you turn your single message into separate quantifiable objectives?

- Why are you using *speech* to communicate your message? Is speech alone the best medium, or do you need visuals and other communication techniques?

- Can you make a clear list of specific *benefits* which your audience will leave with?

3
Understanding and Researching Your Audience

Researching the audience is probably the most neglected aspect of speech preparation. People often spend hours writing and rewriting pages of notes and standing in front of the mirror mouthing words only to make the grave error of forgetting to find out who they will be speaking to.

Aristotle divided the art of oratory into

- the subject matter
- the purpose
- the audience

So the idea of the importance of the audience is not a new one!

Remember, the needs of the audience are paramount.

Some well-repeated classics illustrate what happens when failing to research the audience. They include the man who prepared an after-dinner speech splattered with bawdy jokes at the annual pre-season cricket club dinner, only to discover the evening was not 'stag' and that a certain lady of high moral principles was there. Since his whole speech depended on double-entendres concerning cricket balls, he had to do a rapid rewrite during dinner. Other common errors are preparing a training session or seminar for a group of people who you assume are new employees and fairly naive about management theory only to find that they had attended several of your courses before, and have already heard the kind of 'warm-up' exercises you give to new groups.

One well-known TV personality, who normally charges more than £2,000 for an after-dinner speech, was booed off the platform at a sports association annual dinner for simply reading out clippings from the newspapers (a set piece he repeated at similar occasions) without referring at all to the sport in question, or the occasion.

One of the important pieces of research is to identify what are the **needs** of your target audience—something that many speakers totally ignore.

Advertisers well understand the importance of human needs and drives. They normally start by identifying one fundamental need (such as power, security or social contact) and then try to link the need to the product. We all know that buying a flashy car won't make you more sexy, but if the mind can make a subconscious connection between a Porsche and your sexiness rating then the association is made. If you are aware of the basic and secondary needs of the human animal then you are halfway to understanding your audience and becoming a better communicator.

IDENTIFYING THE NEEDS OF YOUR AUDIENCE

Firstly, no audience will have one single need. You can, however, make certain assumptions based on the common factors of the people making up the audience. Strangely, a large audience tends to react more as a single person than a small group of about 20 people, who tend to react more as individuals. Crowd psychology changes above a certain number.

As we have already seen, advertisers are very aware of the basic and secondary needs of people. So should you be.

Primary needs

Some needs (primary needs) are necessary for life at the most fundamental level. Others (secondary needs) are not *essential* for life but become of prime importance once our basic needs have been satisfied.

Shelter

We need a roof over our head. A good deal of human communication is directed to paying the mortgage, making a nest and making life more comfortable.

Sustenance

We need food to survive. If it tastes and looks nice, so much the better. ('Sell the sizzle, not the steak'.)

Social contact
Hermits aside, we need social contact for healthy living. If locked up in solitary confinement most people will soon start to fall apart mentally, if not physically. The power of touch is very strong and is particularly important in early childhood. We like to be cuddled and feel needed.

Sex and reproduction
As individuals we don't actually *need* sex (the pleasant sensations) for survival. However, the species must reproduce itself or else it dies. Much of our behaviour is part of this instinctive drive to make sure our genes pass on to the next generation, although the conscious motivation for getting married and having children is disguised as something called 'love'.

Security
We need to feel safe and eliminate anxiety. Advertisers, particularly building societies and pharmaceutical companies, play on our need to feel secure and safe from fear.

Survival and self-preservation
The drive to live is very strong. When faced with danger we react by 'flight or fight'. Anything which protects us from danger is very powerful. (Look out for advertisements which play on fear: 'Are *you* covered by insurance if the worst should happen?')

Status and social recognition
This is normally regarded as a secondary need, but some kind of hierarchy is found in the most primitive societies and amongst the animal world. Status and the need to feel important or powerful appears as a key motivator in many advertisements.

Secondary needs
Secondary needs like status are held in the conscious mind, whereas the basic needs are more deeply hidden in our subconscious. Many of the secondary needs follow directly from one basic need. For example, the need to feel powerful and gain control derives from the need for survival.

Abraham Maslow placed human needs in a pyramid starting with the basic **physiological needs** (food, drink, sleep and so on) and **safety needs** at the base and moving up to **self realization** at the apex. The

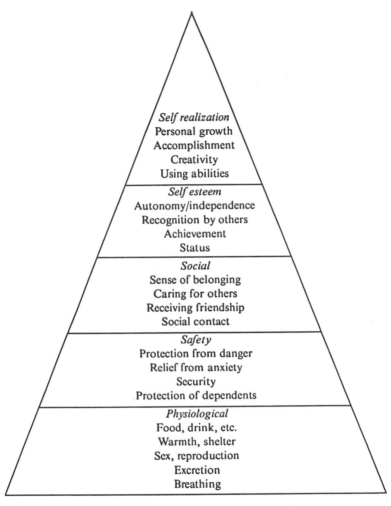

Maslow's hierarchy of needs

idea is that your higher level needs do not become important until the more basic ones are satisfied.

These needs have to be unsatisfied to motivate behaviour. So, if Andy Upwardly-Mobile would like people to think he lives in a trendy warehouse in Docklands and drives a BMW then **status** or **recognition** is his unsatisfied desire. If he flashes the appropriate brand of credit card then perhaps the people he wants to impress might think he's a 'somebody'. Understanding what motivates people is pretty basic stuff. Anyone giving a sales presentation has to understand it—and so should any public speaker.

Example
Now let's apply the 'needs' to an everyday situation.

Suppose you are giving a talk on your Tibetan widgets to an audience of people who are hungry and thirsty. There is no way you are going to interest them unless you can satisfy their need for food and drink first. There are two situations in which hunger and thirst could be the main needs—firstly, where the audience is generally well fed and watered but temporarily in need of sustenance, and secondly, where the audience is in need of food and drink on a more permanent basis (such a group of homeless unemployed). If the drive to find food is a more permanent need (typical of poor communities) then unless you can show how a knowledge of widgets will help them go out and earn lots of money you are onto a loser.

Remember that two of the most powerful human drives are

FEAR and GREED.

There are common errors which are *so* easy to avoid simply by asking some very obvious questions. (In the second half of this Chapter you will find a comprehensive checklist.)

DIFFERENT KINDS OF AUDIENCES

Let's first look at the different types of audiences you might come across and how to identify their particular needs.

Professionals with a high level of knowledge
They might be lawyers attending a conference on new regulations governing the legal profession for instance. Their needs are going to be fairly straightforward. They will have paid a considerable amount to hear about things which are new and pertinent—not the same old stuff they have been learning for years. Their needs are to be educated and informed. The odd joke might be appropriate (legal talks can get very tedious) providing that it relates to the subject. Illustrated material involving slides or video would enhance the presentation but are not essential. The audience should be on your side from the start because it's in their professional interests to be well informed.

Professionals with little previous knowledge

Let's take the same audience but given them a different subject: Marketing. Lawyers will have to learn how to market their services and become more commercially aware following changes in the Law Society regulations which now allow lawyers to advertise. However, lawyers are traditionally professionals not marketeers; the idea of a competitive market place might seem a little strange to a profession where clients normally come by referral or by word of mouth. Your research should therefore try and find out how much previous knowledge they have of marketing concepts and practice. Do they understand terms like the 'marketing mix' or 'database marketing'? How will you set about helping those who are antagonistic to the whole idea of marketing?

University students

Students are assumed to attend lectures in order to pass their exams. However, how many students skip lectures because they can get just as much out of a book? So what are the needs of this audience? If you have attended a lecture you will know that there is a world of difference between a good lecturer and a bad one. A good philosophy lecturer for instance (faced with one of the most difficult subjects) will crystallise, illuminate and stimulate. A bad one will confuse, blabber and ramble.

Teenagers

Now here's a difficult one. Their boredom threshold is very low and motivation even lower. (It's the hormones.) This group is going to need lots of **activities** and **audio-visual aids** to keep them amused; mental stimulation alone isn't enough. The university student aged 20 may be able to handle logical positivism and abstract philosophical concepts, but try this out on a 16-year-old school pupil (or 25-year-old motor vehicle mechanic, or 50-year-old accountant for that matter) and it won't register with them. Teenagers are not for the most part very 'cerebral'.

Prospective buyers

Your aim as a speaker here is quite clear—to persuade your audience to buy. However, each member of the audience may have a different reason for buying. Let's take the situation of buying a time share or holiday ownership. (If you haven't yet succumbed to one of those tempting invitations to win a free Peugeot or spent two hours listening to someone rabbiting on about the joys of buying a timeshare then you must be in the minority). The person giving the presentation has to assume that all his audience have similar needs and tastes in holidays. If you happen to prefer two weeks in the Andes trekking on the back of a llama to five-star luxury in the Bahamas then timeshare isn't really going to suit you. Again, if you can find out about your audience's tastes your job is much easier, and more effective.

Guests at a dinner or wedding

A clear cut situation—or is it? Have you ever heard a best man's speech peppered with mother-in-law jokes fall flat like a lead balloon, or witnessed oblique references to the groom's 'past life' which came as a total surprise to the innocent bride? Again, religious jokes or double entendres about goings on at the stag night won't go down very well if there are several dog collars around the room. Studying the guest list will prevent faux pas.

Members of a women's group

Are they feminists—sisters-in-arms? A lady photographer dressed in dungarees and obviously bra-less, giving a presentation to readers of *Cosmopolitan* magazine at a weekend course on photography started her talk with the words: 'My name is Maggie. I'm a photographer and a feminist' and proceeded to look around the room angrily. Had she looked properly she would have noticed a room full of traditionally dressed ladies with little to suggest a radical outlook on life.

MISJUDGING YOUR AUDIENCE

The most common false assumptions people make about the audience are:

- Assuming they already have some prior knowledge of the subject, when they don't.

- Assuming they know nothing, when they do.

- Assuming that everyone else is interested in what you have to say simply because you are.

- Failing to appreciate the limits of human concentration.

- Failing to appreciate that different kinds of people need different things to stimulate them—words, pictures, feelings and ideas.

• Failing to appreciate the 'hidden agenda'.

Let's take each of these in turn.

Mistake no. 1

Assuming the audience already have some knowledge of the subject when they don't

This is particularly important if you are running a teaching or training session. You can't expect someone to do a three-point turn unless they know how to start the car. Think of the occasions on which you have listened to a lecture or presentation and been totally baffled by the jargon and incomprehensible concepts. Education is full of them. Do you know what TVEI, NCVQ, BTEC and CPVE are? Perhaps you have sat through a 50-minute presentation on education thinking that TVEI was something to do with Television. The world of marketing is equally full of jargon with **fmcg's, SWOTs, dogs** and **stars**.

Hints

1   Use the full version of any abbreviation first. You can always refer to the acronym later. Technical & Vocational Education Initiative (TVEI) is a bit of a mouthful!

2   Have a glossary of terms to hand to save embarrassment—and make sure everyone has a copy.

3   A simple question to the event organiser to establish prior knowledge will avoid you talking above people's heads. For example: 'Do the audience understand Newton's law of gravity?' or 'Will they know what GCSE stands for?'

Mistake no. 2

Assuming the audience know nothing when they do

It is very insulting to an audience to tell them what they already know, it is also a waste of their time, particularly if they have paid to come and hear you. Speaking in a patronising tone of voice is *very* off-putting. If you feel superior to your audience it will come across in the way you talk—and they won't like it! Do always try and tell your audience something new—something they have not heard before. If they are all psychology graduates then all the interesting research about body language and interpersonal communication will come as nothing new, whereas with a group of young management trainees with no academic background (at least not in management or psychology) this area of research could prove fascinating.

Hints

1 Find out the academic background of the audience, or their level within the company if you are addressing them in a professional context.

2 Adopt the approach of 'we are here to share experiences', rather than 'I am here to tell you things'.

3 Testing out their prior knowledge can be done subtly enough with phrases like 'Most of you, of course will be aware...'

Mistake no. 3

Assuming that everyone else is interested in what you have to say simply because you are.

It's the 'local bore' syndrome. Cecil, stalwart of the pub darts team, bird watcher (known as 'twitcher') and Local Authority Accountant finds his work and hobbies fascinating. The trouble is he doesn't realise that no-one else does. He bores everyone to death by rabbiting on about grading levels in the Local Authority Finance Department, recent sightings of Siberian thrushes in Dungeness and how many bull's eyes he scored last night. Enthusiasm may be infectious in some cases but poor Cecil has misunderstood the needs of his audience.

Hints

1 You have to find a common factor with your audience. They are interested in Local Authority Finance because they hate the poll tax. Common enemy—there is your starting point.

2 You may have to take a slightly quirky angle on a boring subject to arouse the interest of the audience. Did you know that in ancient Peru the Spanish used to stand their victims up against a circular board and throw poisoned arrows at them? They didn't—but the story makes pub darts a little more palatable. Do you get the point?

3 Find out what the interests of your audience are. If they are all Local Authority Accountants or twitchers (or twitchy accountants) then you won't have to work so hard.

4 Remember that your audience want to be inspired, enlightened, amused or changed in some way.

Mistake no. 4

Failing to appreciate the limits of human concentration

When was the last time *you* listened to someone speak for a whole hour? A lecture at university, perhaps, or a lesson at school? How much of it did you remember immediately afterwards? How much of it do you remember now? An hour can be an awfully long time. If you go to church, how often have you looked at your watch to see how long the sermon has been going on for? Most sermons last for about 15-20 minutes but can seem much longer.

Most of us remember the *first* few minutes and the *last* few minutes of a speech or talk. This is called the **law of primacy** and the **law of recency**. A concentration curve of an audience listening for about 40 minutes will dip sharply after the first 10 minutes and rise sharply about 3 minutes before the end. Little of the middle section is remembered at all. In Chapter 10 we will be looking at techniques for keeping the audience on their toes and avoiding 'brain dumping'. Let's keep in mind the difficulty the human mind has in concentrating.

Hints

1 Use pointers and signposts to give the audience some framework and structure. (More on this later.)

2 Tell them what you are going to say before you say it, and then tell them you have said it.

3 Use repetition.

4 Use unusual examples, anecdotes and personal stories for reinforcement.

5 Involve your audiences. Ask them questions.

6 Change the pattern of the time slot. Use activities and audio-visual aids.

7 Use your body to illustrate points (within the bounds of decency— Biology teachers take caution!).

8 Use tangible objects as props.

9 Don't be afraid of using sound effects.

10 Vary your delivery in speed, volume, pitch and tone.

All these points will be expanded later in the book.

Mistake no. 5

Failing to appreciate that different people need different things to stimulate them—words, pictures, feelings and ideas.

Understanding an audience means understanding that they are not one person but a collection of individuals who all think, see, hear and feel in different ways. Remember the classic story of the blind man and the elephant? A group of blind men are asked to feel an elephant and guess what they think it is. One says it's a tree (he grabs a leg), another a snake (he grabs the trunk) and another a sword (he grabs the tusk). Have you ever gone to see a film with a friend and come out with totally different experiences? No two people will experience the same thing in the same way.

Research into how we process information in the brain (carried out by two Americans called Bandler and Grinder) shows that people tend to process information visually in pictures, aurally in sounds, kinesthetically in feelings or audio-digitally in semi-abstract thoughts based around words. These models of communication are known as Neuro-Linguistic Programming. They are useful when considering how an audience will react to the same stimulus. Some people react more strongly to pictures, some to sounds, some to feelings and sensations and some to ideas. If the room is hot and stuffy then some people will be affected more than others. If you are using strong visual material, then the visuals will react more positively. The auditory types will tend to hear more than they see and there are others who you will only reach by strong logical reasoning.

To a certain extent this ties in with the theories about the left and right sides of the brain. On the right side of the brain are located the brain cells which deal with creative, visual and spatial processing. On the left side of the brain are located the centres for language processing, mathematics and logical thought. Predominantly right-brained people tend to be 'whole thinkers' (they grasp general concepts rather than detail), they tend to jump from one idea to another with ease, work better in groups, learn better by seeing and doing and are generally creative. Left-brained people tend to think in logical steps, concentrate on the detail rather than broad brush strokes, work better alone and learn better by hearing and thinking. (The reverse is true for left-handed people.)

A public speaker needs to be aware that an audience needs all these different stimuli—visual, auditory, kinesthetic and abstract. If you have an audience of male designers, for instance, they will tend to be predominantly visual and right-brained and you should pepper your presentation with lots of visuals and encourage activity.

If you are teaching someone a foreign language, then you should use different kind of material—visual images, words in books, examples of the spoken language and situations in which people act out situations. You may also find someone who insists that you explain the grammar, in which case you have probably got an 'auditory-digital' left-brain thinker who needs to think through language concepts step by step.

Hints

1 Find out what kind of people will be in the audience—designers, musicians, sales people, accountants, lawyers, for instance. If you have a mixture of lawyers and accountants, then you have probably got an audience of left-brained people. Designers or musicians will tend to be more right-brained, and if they are sales people they could be anything.

2 You won't know how each person processes stimuli, but be aware of pictures, sounds and environmental factors (heat, seating, etc).

Mistake no. 6

Failing to appreciate the 'hidden agenda'

Every meeting has an agenda—a list of items for discussion. The people attending the meeting are supposed to be there to discuss the agenda and come to some decisions. However, their 'hidden agenda' is often the real reason they are there. Here are some hidden agendas:

I am here because I want to chat up the girl in the red dress.

I am here because I want to get away from my parents for the evening.

I am here to pick an argument with x.

I am here because I want to be elected to the Chair for next year.

I am here because there's nothing better to do.

A common failing when talking to over-16s at college or university is that 'they are there because they want to be there'. This also applies to people listening to your after-dinner speech. This may be true, but they may not want to listen to *you*.

We are back to the question of giving the audience what they *want* not what you think they need.

Here is a checklist you should go through before preparing any presentation.

CHECKLIST

How big is the audience?

The size of the group you are addressing will affect the style, content and use of visuals.

5-20. Workshop size
A nice size to work with. You will be able to get away with a flipchart instead of slides or OHP. If you have participation then this shouldn't be a problem. A formal approach with the speaker standing on a podium is probably not suitable.

20-50. Seminar size
This size is more difficult to make participative. You will have to check that everyone can see writing on a flipchart if you decide to use one. Again, if you are planning little-group exercises, with 50 people this is going to take longer than with 25.

50 plus. Conference or lecture size
You're into the big stuff here with platforms, slides and OHPs. An interactive session is going to be difficult to handle unless you split people up into smaller groups.

The implications of group size on use of audio-visual aids will be dealt with later (Chapter 8). For the moment, we just need to bear in mind that group size affects content and style.

What are they expecting?

- A formal lecture or an interactive workshop?
- A serious intellectual talk or a lighthearted anecdotal one?
- Advanced level material or a general introduction?
- An expert speaker or an amateur with a general grasp of the subject?
- Sales patter or objective consideration of pros and cons?
- Facts, figures or general principles?

Problems occur when someone turns up at an interactive workshop dressed in a smart suit only to find that everyone else is in jogging gear ready to lie on the floor and hop about the room. Special problems can arise when you have a group of people completely unfamiliar with the idea of an interactive workshop. There are techniques for loosening people up (mentioned briefly later in this book) but for the moment, just be aware that you will need to find out what the audience are expecting and to prepare them for what you will deliver.

What are they hoping to get out of it?

- An 'altered state' or some kind of dramatic change?
- New information to help them do their job better?
- Help in passing their exams?
- Intellectual stimulation?
- Practical hints on running a business?
- Skill in using the new office database?

Before you even start to research and write your presentation, think: 'At the end of my speech I would like the audience to be able to...' You need to go beyond simple 'understanding'. They must experience a *change* of perception, vision or feeling.

In the last chapter we saw the importance of setting clearly defined objectives as opposed to vague goals. The key factor to remember is that the audience will want to know how to *use* the information and to emerge from your presentation having really learned something useful. This will avoid your speech becoming a 'so what' exercise. John Campbell in his book *Speak for Yourself* (BBC) says, 'The only real measure of our success has to be what the audience will do as a result of our talk.'

What is their previous knowledge?

- Do they understand the basic concepts of, say, financial accounting?
- Have they ever used a wordprocessor before?
- Do they have a general understanding of physiology and anatomy?
- Will they be familiar with paintings by artists such as Renoir or Monet?

This is crucial. One of the worst gaffes you can make is to plunge into something the audience have never heard of, or to offer very simple concepts which they will only find patronising.

If you can't look into this beforehand, then try asking a few simple questions before you start. (This is easy in a small group, but you may find it doesn't work with a large audience.)

What is the age range?

- Will your audience by a mixture of young, old and middle-aged?
- Will you be talking to teenagers?
- Will your audience be mostly retired people?

A relatively homogeneous group in terms of age is going to be easier to prepare for than a wide age range. Jokes and humour date (listen to some of the wartime comedy shows like *Itma*) and language remains exclusive to certain age groups. Do you know what 'megga' means? or what a 'Goth' is? if you don't then this might give away your age?

It's best not to refer to events which might be 'before their time' or to youth cults and sounds that an older audience might not be aware of. Also, age groups share different value systems. The 'baby boomers' (now in their 40s) who lived through the swinging sixties may be more receptive to liberal issues than the 'Thatcher generation' who are in their 20s now and never experienced flower power or the summer of love. But watch for changes—the new generation growing up may be more 'green' than the ageing hippies. And be careful with the teenage years—there is a world of difference between 14 and 16-year-olds!

What is the sex composition of the audience?

- Will the audience be mixed, just men, or just women?

Some people believe that women are a more receptive audience. It's a vast generalisation, but in terms of their openness to new ideas and appetite for knowledge, many speakers find this to be true. Women tend to be more receptive to taking part in communication exercises and more interested in possibilities rather than just 'facts'. If for example you are talking to a group of women about a subject like the paranormal they are likely to be more receptive than a group of men who may poo poo it as being unproven.

Never imagine that an audience of women, such as the local Women's Institute, are just interested in making quilts, baking angel cakes and doing charity work. Women *hate* to be patronised!

If one can risk another generalisation, women tend to lack confidence and are less vociferous in putting across their point of view when men are in the audience. A point to bear in mind with younger audiences is the effect of the opposite sex on how your audience will react—it may inhibit them.

Other things to bear in mind—men are generally more interested in club and sporting activities, making money, the operation of machines and usually think better in terms of logical steps and visual shapes. Women are more intuitive, relate more to words than visual shapes and are more sympathetic to possibilities rather than to facts. These may sound like generalisations but there is in fact substantial research in this area.

What racial or religious groups are being represented?

Race and religion are very sensitive areas. Save your Irish and Jewish jokes for another environment. Be careful how you use racial terms like 'Indian'—some people from the Indian subcontinent or East Africa prefer to be called 'Asian'. Check uncertain words with your key contact who should know the kind of audience you will be addressing. Don't tell Jewish, black or Irish jokes. Avoid racist words like 'coon', 'nigger' or 'Paki'. With certain groups, the word 'black' is banned as being not OK.

Former American President Jimmy Carter managed to offend a number of Polish-Americans in the audience when he tried to play down the controlling effect of Soviet Russia on the other Eastern bloc countries in a pre-election speech. (This was before Glasnost and Perestroika.)

What are the relationships within the audience?

- Do they know each other, or are they all strangers?
- Are there any close relationships?
- What is the status range?
- Will the boss be there?

Picture yourself with an audience you don't know. You are talking about a fairly sensitive subject such as marital breakdown and your audience are really participating well and opening up. You take a coffee break. After the coffee break they suddenly clam up. You were relying on their cooperation in a group exercise and suddenly they won't. What has gone wrong? An additional person has now entered the audience—the company director. Certain people in your audience don't want him to know their dark, intimate secrets.

How to avoid this? You can't necessarily control who is in the audience, but if you are talking about a particularly sensitive subject and need audience participation then you are much safer talking to a group of people who don't work together. You may discover that a particularly influential person is going to be there, and that this may inhibit what is said. If so, a word with that person beforehand might be useful. If they will agree not to let anything said within the room go any further then this will help you enormously.

Other things to watch out for

- Is there a liaison going on between two people?
- Are the people being 'tested' in any way?
- Will you have to report back on their performance?

- Is there likely to be any opposition to what you have to say?
- Are the audience homogeneous in terms of political attitudes?
- Or are you going to be talking to two opposing camps?
- Will you be prepared for arguments rather than a sea of nodding heads?

Will there be any decision makers present?

- Do you know the names of any particular people?

Professional chairmen or women make a point of finding out names of people in the audience and *do their research thoroughly.* You may not use names, but write down a list of about ten names of prominent people in the audience in case you want to refer to them or ask them for comments (a good ploy if attention is flagging or you've forgotten what you were going to say).

Are there likely to be any sensitive issues?
This has been covered briefly in the section on races and religions. Politics is also a sensitive issue.

- What are the politics of the audience? Is it important?
- If the group are homogeneous (an occupational group, for instance) are there any touchy issues?

Professional speakers will advise anyone who is a little unsure of the audience to avoid jokes about sex (unless you are sure it's stag and really know your audience) and race. Political jokes should be chosen carefully. This may sound as if there is nothing much left to talk about, but putting your foot in it will damn you in the eyes of the audience and it will be difficult to retrieve the situation.   If women are present be careful over terms like 'bird' or 'chick'—feminists will get upset. Talking about how to make money from your investments when your audience are left-wing teachers won't go down very well. Nor will praising the virtues of private medicine go down very well with hard-pressed hospital doctors. Be aware of sensitive issues.
    Finally, avoid four letter words at all costs.

What time of day will you be speaking?

- What will have gone before?
- What will their concentration be like after lunch, or at the end of a hard day?

This may not seem very important, but the audience may take on a totally different personality after lunch—the period known as 'the graveyard slot'. Why? Because people have been nicely jollied up with wine and good food and are in no mood to listen to boring old speakers. Recent research suggests that a high protein midday meal with meat will make people perform less well after lunch. That means your audience may not be on top form—and neither will you if you have been gorging yourself with steak and kidney pudding.

The best time of day is probably the second slot of the morning, after the first coffee break, when people are more likely to be receptive. If you are talking during lunch then the speech should be light-hearted. If you are handling a seminar or training session for the whole day, keep your workshop and participatory exercises to early afternoon and late morning. People don't take in much just before lunch because they are hungry and the adrenalin should be nicely flowing just after lunch.

The end of the day is a bad time because people are thinking of getting home. Always finish promptly. Remember that evening sessions should be more light-hearted than day sessions.

People listen better on a full stomach but not after booze. Students, if they have just come from an hour's typing class or a formal logic lecture may be in no mood to tackle a dry subject. Friday afternoons are bad times for learning generally. Bad news won't make your audience receptive if they are in an agitated state. They may need to release their frustration before you start. For example, if you are addressing a local group on the benefits of the poll tax and they have just heard that it's set at £500 per head they won't be very receptive to what you have to say. Relieve their anger first by dealing with direct questions.

Watch the news. Talking to a group of people about pensions and taxation when the Chancellor has just announced changes will make you look a little silly. Talking about legal matters when there is a Bill going through Parliament you had no knowledge of will leave you with egg on your face. There will always be *someone* better informed than you.

This brings us to the next question.

What is their attitude likely to be?

- Will they be hostile or favourable—or divided?
- Will they want to listen?
- Will they view you as a hostile speaker?
- Will you be seen as having credentials as an expert or as an amateur with something to say?

If your credibility is in doubt, then you will either have to say a few words (or get the chairman to do it for you) about your background, or say you are there as a non-specialist with something to say.

EXERCISES

You are preparing a talk on computers and what they can do for two different audiences. (a) A group of women returning to work who have no previous knowledge. (b) A group of schoolboys aged 17 who may have a fair bit of knowledge already. They are taking computer studies as a general study in the 6th form.

State:

(1) your main objective(s) for each group;
(2) what prior knowledge you would assume;
(3) what questions you would need to ask before you spoke to the two groups.

Example

Read this explanation of what a computer does and assess its relevance to each group.

'The X computer uses hard or soft discs and may have separate or built-in disc drives. Some versions operate by using a mouse, others have function and command keys. All of them have VDUs. Any software designed for DOS 2 will run on this machine. Data is output to an EGA screen and a dot matrix printer. The computer can be linked to others in the system by means of a modem. It can store 40 megabytes of information and is very user friendly.'

Rewrite this to make sense of it for both audiences. Remember, one group knows nothing and one group knows a little.

If you find it too difficult, try explaining how a microwave works to someone who has never seen one before, for example a group of refugees.

CHECKLIST

Have you checked the following?

— Size of audience
— Sex ratio
— Racial and religious groups
— Level of knowledge
— Expectations
— Attitudes
— Homogeneity

— Age range—social and cultural background
— Occupational mix
— Sensitive issues
— Time of day
— Precedents
— Venue

Answers to exercises on page 16

(1) News of redundancies to a workforce of about 1,000.
Because of the size of the group, the news cannot easily be announced verbally to a thousand people at once. However, those people being made redundant should be told personally face-to-face and then receive a letter outlining the terms. The rest of the workforce who are retaining their jobs could then be informed by letter. The important point to remember is that rumours should not be given time to circulate.

(2) Launch of a new product on the market to an audience of press retailers.
Speech is obviously the best medium of communication. This can then be followed up by media coverage (eg: the trade press) and publicity material sent to the press and retailers.

(3) Condolences to a friend on losing their spouse.
This needs to be done by personal handwritten letter. In certain circumstances condolences can be conveyed verbally face-to-face if the person is a very close friend.

(4) Instructions to a group of novices on how to sail a boat.
Instructions should be given verbally to the group using the boat to illustrate, or using diagrams and illustrations.

(5) The life and work of Vincent van Gogh to the local arts society.
This merits an illustrated talk with slides.

(6) Explaining a new office communications system to office staff.
A verbal explanation with overhead transparencies backed up with handouts and written instructions.

(7) Health and Safety procedures to staff.
Noticeboards should be placed in strategic positions (especially near relevant equipment and fire exits). The procedures should also be disseminated by written memo and a verbal briefing session may be necessary for small groups.

(8) Explaining the National Curriculum to teachers nationally.
The national media should be used (press, radio and television) plus conferences and training sessions.

(9) Notice of an emergency meeting to be held at 24 hours' notice.
The telephone or fax machine are the quickest ways of getting in touch with people.

(10) Instructions to various isolated platoons in a desert army.
Some possibilities include Morse code, radio telephones, or any short distance electronic communication devices. In previous times other methods were used—personal courier on horseback, burning beacons, semaphore, etc.

4
Preparing Your Speech

The key to successful presentation is **preparation**. Almost every book which has been written on the subject rightly dwells on the importance of preparation, research and structure.

But how do you start?

GETTING IDEAS

Let's suppose you are a careers officer and have been asked to give a talk on 'Choosing a career' at a local school. Your audience will be composed of 15 and 16-year-olds who may (or may not) be interested in their future career. You will have already thought through what the needs of that audience are—to be stimulated, entertained, enlightened and given some specific information and help as well.

In front of you is a blank sheet of paper. You start jotting down some category headings—school subjects, parents' influence, opportunities, and so on—and then you reach a mental block. How on earth can you make this sound stimulating? You need to start all over again. The problem is that you have imposed a structure already and set your brain moving along one narrow track. You may be very organised but, at this stage, that is the *last* thing that you need to be.

Creative thinking

Original ideas and unusual approaches come from the random connection of thoughts. The brain does not work in a 'logical' pattern: if you start by writing an outline then you are imposing order before you have had a chance to generate *ideas*. Imagine your brain as a growing tree. It doesn't develop in a linear fashion—branches start sprouting and then other branches and twigs appear and so on. Just as a tree doesn't grow by starting with the trunk and then going on to branch number one and then branch number two, so our brain develops in a rather random way. If you use the brainstorming and mind-mapping methods (explained later) then you will learn to think in a more creative way and the ideas will flow. *Then* you can start to impose a structure later.

If you are a *left brain* thinker— logical, scientific, strategic—then you may find the following methods a little strange because you have not been used to using the *right side* of your brain—the creative, artistic, spatial and random side. Ideally, you should learn to use both sides.

Agatha Christie's character Miss Marples is an excellent example of a person with perfect balance between the left, logical thinking brain and the right, lateral thinking brain. Unlike the police inspectors, portrayed as slightly stupid because they take the obvious, logical approach to detection and end up in a blind alley, Miss Marple's brain operates in a more random way. She operates by making connections between two apparently unrelated observations. The connection is often made in a flash, with the super-sleuth gazing into space with the words, 'Yes of course, quite so', a brilliant lateral thinker.

Edward de Bono, famous for his books and lectures on 'lateral thinking' suggests this method for getting the brain to work in a creative, lateral way. Take a subject on which you are preparing a speech, pick a word at random from the dictionary and then try and make a connection between the two, even if it sounds stupid.

Let's now try some brainstorming ourselves.

Brainstorming

Brainstorming is a method of generating ideas using *free association*. Creative teams in advertising agencies often use it to come up with new and original ideas for commercials. It can also be done as a solo activity. Essentially, the principle is to start with a word, say the theme of a talk, and to write down the next idea or word that comes into your head. In group sessions, no comment must be made on the suitability of the word or idea—it is simply noted and the next person carries on.

Try it yourself as a solo exercise with the theme word TOURISM. Write down any words or images that you associate with this word. Form a chain—all your words won't necessarily relate to the original word TOURISM. Even if you seem to be heading in a totally unfamiliar direction and going off the point, follow your thoughts down this channel.

Now try it with the word CAREERS and see what happens. If you find the exercise difficult, then put yourself in a relaxed position and fix your eyes on something. What will happen is that you will begin to put yourself in a semi-trance state which will encourage left brain thinking. It is no coincidence that some of the most original ideas come to people in the 'daydream' state between sleeping and waking. (More on this later in the Chapter.)

Now you are ready to put down your ideas on paper.

Mind-mapping

Mind-mapping was developed in the 1970s by the academic Tony Buzan and has been widely adopted in study skills manuals. It uses the technique of brainstorming to generate ideas which are then 'mapped' on paper. The idea is to get the two sides of the brain—the logical and creative—to work together to generate ideas. Like a growing tree, the method hinges around seeing how ideas branch off from single themes and connections can be made. It also utilises both words and pictures. (Pictures are easier to remember.)

You will just need a plain piece of paper and several coloured pens.

Step one
Write your topic in the centre of the page:

CHOOSING A CAREER

Step two
Now start writing down words which come into your head (or you can draw pictures if you wish) around the page.

ACADEMIC   SUBJECTS   PERSONALITY
MOTIVATION   OPPORTUNITIES   UNIVERSITY
PARENTS' INFLUENCE   SKILLS   TESTS etc.

Step three
Go back to each word and write down *secondary* words which come to mind for each of the key words. For example, your key word is PERSONALITY. Your secondary words could be PERSUASIVE, HELPING, INTROVERTED, CONTROLLING, SHY, etc. Don't worry if they don't seem totally logical at this point.

Step four
Now start joining up the key words or pictures using lines. Start with lines radially from the central theme CHOOSING A CAREER.

Step five
Take your different coloured pens and underline words which are

related in the same colour. Alternatively, you can put a number or letter by each word or phrase that falls into the same category.

Step six
Try joining up all the other words as illustrated in the diagram.

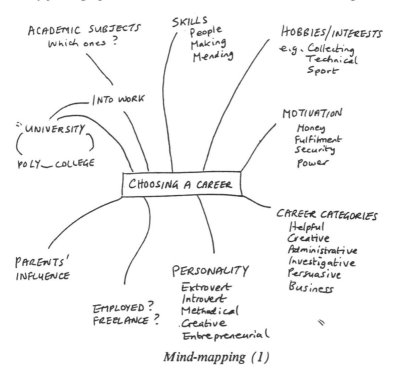

Mind-mapping (1)

What you have been doing is using the right side of the brain initially to generate ideas using free association, and then the left side to organise those ideas.

Substitute the word of your own choice—a career with which you are familiar and try the exercise yourself. An example is overleaf.

Now try the same exercise with the name of a sport—HOCKEY, CRICKET or FOOTBALL, for instance. Imagine you are speaking at a club dinner. See what ideas come from the mind-mapping method.

The logic behind this method is that it reproduces the way the brain works. If you could see the network of millions of interconnections inside the brain it would look like a gigantic telephone exchange. Every time learning takes place, another connection is made between

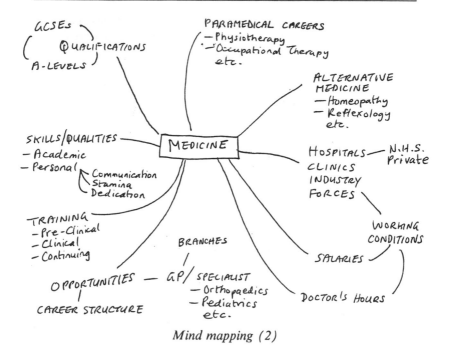

Mind mapping (2)

two nerve endings. The brain makes sense of new information and sensory data by using its existing framework to slot it into a category. Eventually, when enough new stimuli present themselves, new categories are created.

If you find this method alien, there's no need to force yourself to do it. Instead, try some relaxation exercises, and try to develop your own way of generating and recording ideas.

Creativity and relaxation exercises

Sometimes people get mental blocks. It's the blank piece of paper syndrome. An executive typically spends about 24 hours in total preparing a presentation lasting about three-quarters of an hour. During that time numerous pieces of paper get crumpled and thrown in the bin. What goes wrong?

You may not be in an environment conducive for generating ideas. Take yourself back to the schoolroom—hard chairs, uninspiring decoration, sterile atmosphere. No wonder people find it hard to produce good work in those surroundings. You may have come up with your best ideas lying on a sofa listening to Bach or sitting in a train gazing out of the window.

The right side of the brain (the creative side) responds better to certain rhythms, for example, the slow beat of Baroque music like J S Bach and Vivaldi, or the chuggerty-chug of a train. Sit yourself in a comfortable position, put on some Baroque music and start to dream. You may find that you fall into a semi-trance state where the highly suggestible subconscious starts to become active. Try it. Another good time to jot down ideas is just before you go to sleep. Put a note pad and pen beside your bed and write down any good ideas that come into your head.

All these methods for generating ideas using both sides of the brain are important when actually delivering the speech. If people in your audience are stimulated into using both sides of their brain and receive a multi-sensory experience, what you say will stay in their memory longer.

RESEARCH

Let's look now at researching the content of your presentation. In some cases, what you want to say comes straight out of your head without any trouble. In other cases you may have to do some research—find quotations, anecdotes and topical news stories, for example.

Let's take the subject of the careers talk again and narrow it down to one area: JOURNALISM. Your audience consists of 15-year-olds who have expressed an interest in careers in the media. How should you do your research? What will they want to know?

Essentially, they will need to know:

- how to become a journalist;
- whether they will need particular qualifications;
- tips of getting in 'through the back door';
- what kinds of jobs are available;
- what skills a journalist needs;
- what the life of a journalist is like, etc.

You will need information on courses available, routes into the profession and tips from practising journalists about getting started. Basically, research sources are divided into **primary** and **secondary** sources. Primary sources means people with whom you have direct contact, by letter, telephone or face-to-face, in other words getting information 'straight from the horse's mouth'. Secondary sources are almost always written—books, newspapers, reports and so on. To make your speech interesting don't use just one source of formation: get a balance between your own experiences, objective facts and stories from other people's experiences.

Primary sources

— Personal contacts and friends
— Your own experiences
— Face-to-face interviews
— Telephone interviews
— Anything not written down or printed

Secondary sources

— Books
— Newspapers, magazines and journals
— Reports, surveys and other printed information
— Museums, galleries, building, shops—objects rather than words
— Visual sources—films, TV, photographs, etc
— Auditory sources—radio, records/tapes, etc
— Companies and organisations (who can provide information in any of the forms mentioned)

At the end of the book you will find a list of useful sources and bibliography of information and references.

Taking the subject of a careers talk on **journalism** for example, you will need to find an up-to-date book on careers in journalism, telephone the Newspaper Society or Periodical Training Trust to check your facts on training courses, telephone several publications to get a 'feel' for the kind of young people they are looking for.

For other subjects you could use a set of reference books. Try a book of quotations such as the *Oxford Dictionary of Quotations*, a book of anecdotes and stories such as *The 637 Best Things Anybody Ever Said* or *The Book of Heroic Failures* and a book of useful and useless facts like *100% British* or *The Book of Averages* are invaluable (details in the bibliography at the end of this book). Encyclopaedias and dictionaries are useful if you want potted histories or definitions.

Some professional speechmakers keep a file of newspaper cuttings—for example on strange true tales and double entendres. Such things can come in very useful—comb the diary section in the daily newspapers for anecdotes.

STRUCTURING THE PRESENTATION

Now we come onto the crucial phase of preparation—getting the right structure for your talk. We'll assume that you already have a list of headings and ideas.

'Expert' speechmakers and advisers on presentations disagree over the important of structure. There is the school, represented by David Bernstein, author of *Put it together, Put it across*, which says that the structure is everything. Bernstein says: 'Before I put it across I need to put it together'. Other experts say that 'it's not what you say, it's the way that you say it'. Michael Gelb, author of *Present Yourself*, says that the audience will tend to focus more on the body language and rhythm of the voice than on the content.

Whichever point of view you adopt, for the inexperienced speaker, structure is crucial because it gives you the security of a plan.

Let's go through the steps you now need to take, to turn your disconnected ideas into an organised structure.

Three steps to a structured presentation

Step one: identifying the core statement
Identify your main proposition. What *single* thing are you trying to get across? What is your conclusion going to be? Try phrasing something in quantifiable objectives. For instance, 'At the end of my presentation I would like you each to go away knowing exactly how a school leaver can embark upon journalism training, what is involved and what opportunities are open to journalism. I would also like to inspire each of you a little'. (See pages 19-20 for the section on forming objectives.)

Step two: setting objectives
Identify your main objectives/elements and sub-elements. You should have between 3 and 6 main in total, preferably no more. Your talk could for example cover the following:

A. Qualifications
   (1) Entry for graduates
   (2) Entry for school leavers
   (3) Other ways in.

B. Different kinds of journalism
   (1) Newspapers
   (2) General magazines
   (3) Trade press
   (4) Radio and TV
   etc

At this stage don't worry too much whether the points are in the right order.

Step three: the framework
You need a route map or framework. Are you going to start at the beginning and go through historically? Would it be better to start with a proposition, then discuss pros and cons before coming to a conclusion? Or might it be better to start with a problem, then discuss research methodology before evaluating findings and summing up?

Which framework you choose depends very much upon the nature of the subject matter and the purpose of your communication. Here are the main structures you could choose from:

- for and against (pros and con)
- persuasive form (problem and solution)
- the classical form (stages and recapitulations)
- the scientific form
- the historical form
- geographical form
- categories
- dramatic narrative

Let's explore each one in turn.

For and against or pros and cons

- Outline of issue
- Arguments for (or against)
- Summary of arguments
- Arguments against (or for)
- Summary of arguments
- Recap of issues
- Conclusion—food for thought or hard hitting persuasive point

This is the classic debating society format and probably the one with which you are most familiar. It is also the format used in the legal system. First you get the case for the prosecution, then the case for the defence. You have probably written essays along the lines of 'Discuss the reasons for and against the legislation of soft drugs' or something similar. The idea basically is to present the arguments and let the audience make their own mind up, or come to some conclusion with the purpose of persuading them to a certain point of view.

This format is normally used for seminars in which you are asked to present arguments for and against a proposition and invite the audience to make up their own mind. It is also used for talks about objective subjects like careers talks to school pupils and situations which require the **presentation of a balanced argument**. For example, you are presenting to a tutorial group at university the arguments for and against some political/academic/legal issue such as whether the A-level examination system should be reformed.

Your approach should differ according to the type of audience you are speaking to. If it is less well educated than yourself, subordinate to you in status, with low self-esteem and a sympathy with your message, then you need only present one side of the argument. However, if your audience is well educated, of high status and possibly not in sympathy with your message, then you should put both points of view by presenting them with a challenge and identifying the benefits.

This leads us onto the second structure.

Persuasive form or problem and solution

- Outline purpose or problem/paint a scenario
- Problems/reasons against
- Demolish reasons against—the 'product' is the solution
- Outline benefits/reasons for
- Summarise benefits
- Conclusion—action or selling point.

This is similar to the 'for and against' structure, except the purpose is not to expostulate and present a balanced picture but to change attitudes or influence. The structure is subtly different and the language will be much more emotive. Analyse the structure of a television commercial:

> Picture of harassed woman doing the washing (scenario)
> 'Can't get all those nasty stains out?' (problem)
> 'Powders XYZ just won't shift them' (demolish opposition)
> 'Try BLOB—the powder with a difference...' (benefits)
> 'Remember that BLOB removes all the deep-rooted stains that other powders leave behind' (summary)
> 'Buy BLOB' (action)

This structure is the classic one used by sales professionals. Often step two (reasons against) will be skipped—not always wise as the audience will always have objections in their mind. One common technique is to take a market such as package holidays and outline the main problems or anxieties people have—not being able to get to the place they want, awful hotels and food, resort not all it's cracked up to be, too expensive, etc. If this sounds familiar it's the technique commonly used by people trying to sell time-share or holiday ownership. They put problems in people's minds and then produce this wonderful time-share 'product' to solve all their problems.

One thing you should *not* do (mentioned in Chapter 5) is to say: 'I am going to convince you that buying a time-share will save you money and...'. You will persuade best by suggestion and enticement.

The 'persuasive' format works for any situation in which you are essentially persuading people to a course of action—to change the way they do things, to introduce a new subject to the curriculum, to buy a product, to run an event.

The classical form (like sonata form in classical music)

- Outline/introduction (can take the form of questions)
- Stage 1 or opening theme
- Recapitulation of 1
- Stage 2 or second theme
- Recap of 1 and 2
- Stage 3 or development section
- Recap of 1, 2 and 3
- Conclusion

Basically this is 'Tell them what you're going to say. Then say it. Then tell them you've said it.'

This fits well in situations where you want to convey information or instruct. For example, you may be teaching people the principles of sailing before you let them loose on a boat; it is important that they remember each step in turn before they hoist the sail and set off.

You don't, of course, have to stick to three points, but research has shown that people remember best in threes, and after that in fives and sevens and tens—but not twos, fours and sixes, for some totally mysterious reason.

The scientific form

- Purpose of study, question to be investigated
- Method of investigation
- Date used
- Findings
- Conclusions – QED

This structure is most commonly used in the academic world especially the sciences and social sciences. For example, suppose you are involved in a survey to discover the awareness of university students of AIDS, how it spreads, and how to keep yourself from catching it. You start by outlining the proposition which includes several points for investigation such as 'To investigate how many university students think that AIDS originated from green monkeys in Africa.' The next step is to outline the method of investigation— questionnaire given to random sample of 100 males and 100 females between ages 18 and 21 plus in-depth interviews with 25 males and 25 females. And so on. Your conclusion is a statement of the findings: 'That 90% of males and 5% of females believe that the AIDS virus originates from green monkeys in Africa.'

Historical/chronological structure

- Stage 1 – the infant (0-1)
- Stage 2 – the toddler (1-5)
- Stage 3 – early school days (5-7)
- Stage 4 – juniors (7-11)
- Stage 5 – Teenagers (12-19) etc

This structure works best for historical talks or for subjects which fit into developmental phases. It is probably the easiest structure to master as it follows an obviously logical sequence. Other subjects which fit neatly into this structure are talks about the history of a building and talks relating to problems occurring over time.

Geographical and spatial

- Europe or EEC
- Eastern Europe
- The Middle East
- The Pacific Basin

This is the obvious one to use when talking about cultural topics or about any geographical or travel subjects. If you are talking about a building, then starting with one room and talking your audience through room by room is one approach. Other structures can be used for both kinds of subject such as grouping countries and regions according to languages, (the English-speaking countries), or climate (tropical, desert, temperate and so on—see next section).

Categories/lists

- English
- Spanish
- Arabic

- Chinese
- Latin

These are all ways of grouping languages according to their root. Other subjects that fit easily into the categories or list format are occupational groups, social and lifestyle groups. Advertising and marketing people seem to love categories!

Here are some examples:

'Fast moving consumer goods'—food, drink, household, etc.
'Consumer durables'—fridges, cars, etc.
'YUPPIES'—young upwardly-mobile professionals.

The idea is to divide up your main points and go through each one step by step as in American-style management seminars.

Example: 'The *ten* golden rules for success.'

Dramatic narrative

- Set the scene/arouse interest
- Introduce the characters or theme of the plot
- Develop the plot
- Climax
- And the moral of the tale is...

This is the oldest form of communication. Newspaper journalists still call news reports 'stories' although a news story has a slightly different format beginning with a hard hitting point and tailing off towards the end.

It is difficult to give a structure here. It's best to tell something as it happened, let the story unfold and keep the audience on their toes by building suspense and leaving the 'punch line' until the end.

The story telling structure can be incorporated into other formats—you can have a short story as part of a general talk.

There are other structures but the ones we have discussed should offer an answer to most public speaking needs.

Exercise

Take the subject of CARNIVAL. You are a student of Art & Design and have been set a project to do on the origins of and practices associated with carnival. You do your brainstorming and write your ideas down in the form of a mind-map that might look something like the one opposite.

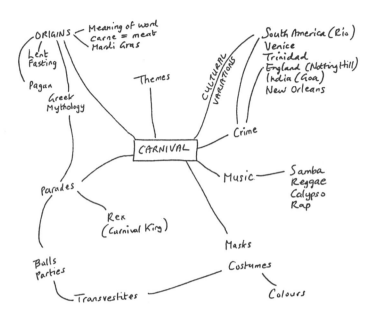

Mind-mapping (3)

Starting to organise these key words you might come up with a structure that is a mixture of chronological and spatial forms:

A. Origins of carnival　　　　　　　　– Lenten traditions, Mardi Gras
　　　　　　　　　　　　　　　　　　– meaning of the word (carne = meat)

B. Ancient carnivals
C. European/Latin carnivals　　　　　– Venice, Spain, etc
D. South American/Latin carnivals – Rio
E. Black/West Indian carnivals　　　 – Trinidad, Notting Hill

Step four: liven it up a bit
You have your structure and you have organised your points into some logical order (which may change when you write it). You will need some anecdotes, illustrations, quotations and perhaps a few jokes (chosen with care) to pepper up your speech. These can be slotted in at appropriate spots. Avoid just following the structure step

by step: it would become terribly boring! (See Chapter 5 for some suggestions on anecdotes and see the bibliography for suitable reference books.)

Step six
You are ready to start writing.

CHECKLIST

— Have you identified an appropriate structure?

— Does it fit with the subject matter?

— Are your ideas thought out properly? Do you know what you are trying to put across?

— Will the structure be easy for the audience to follow?

— Are you organising your ideas in logical sequence or the most sensible progression? If not (assuming that a sequential structure is not the most appropriate) does your structure use dramatic narrative or make sense in another way?

— Have you fulfilled your core statement?

— Are your facts thoroughly checked?

'I need something to help me overcome my
personal verbosity situation.'

5
Writing Your Speech

Now you are ready to put pen to paper, or finger to wordprocessor. Most people, including some of the most experienced raconteurs, write their speeches down, even if they then transfer the words to cue cards or speak extempore.

Writing your speech out in full is a useful exercise, even for experienced speakers, for two reasons. Firstly, it helps to organise all your thoughts. Secondly, if you are still stuck for ideas, the actual process of writing will help your creative buds to produce inspiration.

Drafting a speech step by step
The recommended steps are:

- first, write a rough draft;
- second, refine your draft, adding illustrations and changing words;
- third, rewrite it into *spoken* English, shortening sentences and changing words;
- fourth, rehearse the speech aloud, timing it; and
- fifth, make alterations in order to fit the time slot.

We are going to look now at how to use language to communicate effectively in speech, how to make an impact at the beginning and bring the presentation to a suitable close. Finally, once you have written your speech you will then learn how to transfer this to cue cards or other prompt devices.

Learn how to 'write like a good talker' and 'think like a listener'. (David Bernstein, *Put it together, put it across*.)

THE USE OF LANGUAGE IN SPEECH

Language is simply a code which conveys meaning. Like morse code or semaphore it works because the sender and receiver of the communication understand similar meanings for the same words—or at least they should do.

Your choice of language is crucial if you are to make contact with your audience. If you use too much jargon to a 'lay' audience you will lose them. If you use formal language with a group of teenagers you will send them off to sleep. If you speak English in a pompous, written style then people will switch off. Language is the main tool by which you communicate your ideas and facts to the audience. However, the response of the audience will depend very much upon how you use that language. Simply *telling* people facts will fail because it won't affect their *emotions* or meet their *needs*. Facts need to be dressed up for the audience to remain interested and to remember what you have said.

The main errors of language that speechwriters make are:

1. Writing an essay and then reading it without translating it into spoken English.

2. Being too long-winded and using long sentences.

3. Not understanding how to use repetition and rhythm.

4. Failing to give the audience frequent signposts to tell them where the speaker is heading.

5. Failing to use rhetorical questions and the word YOU.

6. Failing to harness the emotive power of words.

7. Overuse of clichés and redundant language.

8. Using jargon and abbreviations that people don't understand.

9. Failing to use anecdotes, quotations and illustrations to add colour.

10. Overusing dry facts and statistics without making analogies and using colourful illustrations.

11. Failing to consider the limits of memory of the audience.

So what should you bear in mind when writing a speech?

ELEVEN GOLDEN RULES

1. Use spoken rather than written English

What is oral style and why should you use it?
The commonest error of the inexperienced speechmaker is to write

down their speech and then read it with their head buried in the paper. The audience immediately feels that the speaker is not talking *to* them but *at* them. Experienced speakers, politicians included, often *do* read speeches, but they still manage to make them sound as if they are just speaking from notes. Newscasters have to be able to read from an autocue whilst making it appear that they are talking directly to the viewers. (At the end of this chapter are examples of radio and television scripts for you to read as an exercise.) Don't write your notes in long sentences; they be too difficult to get your tongue around.

Look at the way advertisements are written. They break most of the rules of grammar, starting sentences with 'And' for instance and they use a very chatty style. Take a look at this extract from an advertisement for Ovaltine:

Yes, Ovaltine can be drunk for breakfast.

And why not? It's made, is it not, from barley, malt extract and eggs. What better for setting you up for the day?... In fact, a mug of Ovaltine provides most of the nutrients required by the body.

And Ovaltine contains no added sugar, no artificial flavour, colour or preservatives.

Formidable! Eh? Mind you, if Ovaltine is such a good source of energy how come we Brits drink it before bed?

This is English written to be *read out loud*—and it is an example of the kind of style you should use when writing your speech.

To show you how stilted written English can sound when spoken aloud, try reading aloud this passage from *The Student Book* (Macmillan) on studying Chemistry:

"Chemistry is an area of study which touches human life at innumerable points. It is the science which forms a bridge between physics and biology as well as between earth sciences and life and medical sciences. It is therefore a **central science** which holds the key to an appreciation and understanding of life-cycles on the one hand through to man-made processes on the other.

The development of chemistry as a science has taken pace at an increasingly rapid rate over the last two centuries, and has depended upon **quantitative** reasoning. Chemists of the nineteenth century could not have anticipated the contribution which their research would make to the applications of chemistry today—applications which range from micro-circuits and developments in solid state devices to the use of hormones as a new generation of pesticides, and which even give a glimmering of understanding of the chemical basis of life itself. In many cases this rapid progress in the application of chemistry has itself created new crises for man (eg: some forms of pollution; the effect of some pesticides on the environment, or the side effects of some pharmaceuticals), but chemists have immediately led the search for an answer to the resulting problems so that the advances could be controlled or harnessed to the benefit of man.

Superficially it is fairly easy to visualise the earth in terms of basic chemical concepts—it is an apparent equilibrium between solid, liquid and vapour phases surrounded by space and supplied with energy from the sun. However, the apparent position of the equilibrium is continually moving and small changes have profound effects on the processes of life..."

So why doesn't it work as a piece of English to be spoken aloud?

- The sentences are too long. Take the one which starts: 'Superficially it is fairly easy to visualise...'

- Some of the language is too complicated. It can't all be taken in at once (solid state devices, micro-circuits, etc).

- There are no pointers or linking words like 'however'. 'firstly' and 'although'. It would need phrases to coax the audience into the next points, like: 'Let's look at some of the practical uses of chemistry... Firstly...'.

- There is no reference to the needs of the audience, or the word YOU.

When you *read* such a passage, you can take it at your own pace, go back and read bits again. When it is *spoken*, you lose most of it once it's been said.

Try reading a piece from a newspaper and see how it sounds. Try re-writing the piece for a radio news bulletin (example on page 98).

Here are the main points to bear in mind when writing English to be spoken aloud.

- Use 'You've' instead of 'You have' and other such abbreviations. See how clumsy this sounds: 'I have come here today to tell you why you are making the wrong decision and why you cannot pursue this course of action.' Use 'I've', 'you're' and 'can't'.

- Use positive speech. Don't say: 'I am not here today to persuade you to choose accountancy as a career, nor will I try and tell you that it isn't boring, sometimes.'

- Use active not passive sentences. Don't say: 'The rules of the common room have been changed by the school governors.' Say 'The school governors changed the common room rules.'

- Use direct speech. Avoid the use of the pronoun 'One'. Hear how stilted it sounds. 'When one goes to the races one often makes a bet, doesn't one?' Use the word *you*—it makes direct contact with your audience. Incidentally, try and avoid too much reference to yourself and limit the use of the word 'I'.

- Don't write numbers (ie figures) into your speech. Write them out in full. For example, 1,797,021 is much easier to say if you write one million, seven hundred and ninety-seven thousand and twenty-one. (There will be more on using facts and statistics in point 10.)

- Keep sentences short. They have more impact. They are more forceful. People cannot (can't) remember long sentences.

- If in doubt, write as if for a reader of *The Sun* not *The Times*.

This brings us onto point number two—the question of sentence construction.

2. Use short sentences and vary the structure
A sentence consists of a number of words strung together with a subject and a verb. Generally, sentences do one of the following: make a statement, make a wish, ask a question, instruct or command, or make some kind of exclamation. How you *arrange* the words is called **syntax**—and the order can completely change the meaning.

What should we consider when writing sentences for speech?

- **Sentences should normally be short.**

  Forget about sub-clauses and long sentences. Where you would normally write one long sentence, speak it in three short ones. For example, here is a perfectly constructed sentence with a subordinate clause:

  'The cat, which had just licked its saucer of milk clean of every final scrap, curled up into a fluffy ball of ginger fur, licked its lips and fell asleep on the mat.'

Translated into *spoken* English, this would read: 'The cat licked its saucer clean of milk. It curled up into a ginger fluffy ball. And finally, it licked its lips and fell asleep on the mat.'

Go back to the extract on Chemistry. This will be easier to read if rewritten as:

'Superficially it is fairly easy to imagine the earth in terms of basic chemical concepts. The earth is an apparent equilibrium between three phases. These are—solid, liquid and vapour. The three phases are surrounded by space and supplied with energy from the sun.'

- **Sentences should vary in length**

Try and keep your sentences to between 5 and 15 words as a general rule. Longer sentences *can* work but only if they run before or after short sentences.

Consider this example from a speech by Victor Hugo on the centenary of the death of Voltaire:

'A hundred years ago today a man died. He died immortal. He departed laden with years, laden with the most illustrious and fearful of responsibilities, the responsibility of the human conscience informed and rectified...'

- **Put the key words at the end of a sentence**

This will make the audience anticipate your key word or point. Take these two sentences:

'The National Westminster Bank in the City of London is the tallest building in Britain.'

This would have more impact if rephrased as: 'The tallest building in Britain is ... the National Westminster Bank in the City of London.'

- **Make use of parallelism, antithesis, inversions and balanced construction, where appropriate**

Constructing a sentence with two distinct halves can make an impact. Here are some examples:

'It is nothing to die; it is frightful not to live.' (Victor Hugo).

'Life is rather like a tin of sardines—we're all of us looking for the key.' (Alan Bennett in *Beyond the Fringe*).

'Life is a tragedy when seen close-up, but a comedy in long shot.' (Charlie Chaplin).

'Ask not what your country can do for you. Ask what you can do for your country.' (John F. Kennedy *Inaugural address*, 1961).

'Life is a great play. The final act is a tragedy.' (Cicero).

- **Use a string of powerful adjectives for impact**

Study these two examples:

'You betray it [your baptism] by drunkenness, gluttony, anger, revenge.' (John Wesley).

'I have nothing to offer but blood, toil, tears and sweat.' (Winston Churchill).

Other structures which can be effective are sentences constructed in three parts, which make three succinct points. This brings us onto the question of repetition and rhythm.

3. Use repetition and rhythm

People like to hear words that have a rhythmic feel, particularly if they come in threes. They also like repetition because it gives them a structure. Consider these extracts from well-known speeches:

'There are some of us, Mr Chairman, who will fight and fight and fight again to save the Party we love.' (Hugh Gaitskell, Labour Party Conference, Scarborough, 1960).

'*I have a dream* that my four little children will one day live in a nation where they will not be judged by the colour of their skin but by the content of their character. *I have a dream today. I have a dream* that one day the state of Alabama, whose governor's lips are presently dripping with words of interposition and nullification, will be transformed into the situation where little black boys and black girls will be able to join hands with little white boys and white girls and walk together as sisters and brothers. *I have a dream* today. *I have a dream* that one day ... etc. (Martin Luther King, 1963).

Just reading this speech it can seem like a bad example of over-sentimentality. Hearing Luther King *speak* it, however, is a different matter. Note the use of long words like 'interposition' and 'nullification' which refer, in a derogatory way, to the Governor of Alabama. See how the simple words 'little black boys and little black girls' seem so sincere after that verbiage. Note, again, the use of repetition.

Many speakers have used 'the rules of threes'—making three short statements that have a rhythm. Try and think of well-known phrases or quotations that come in threes (the magic figure) like 'Liberty, equality, fraternity.' It doesn't sound quite so effective in fours and twos, but fives and sevens are almost as effective. If there is anything that is almost guaranteed to make the audience break out into applause it is a string of three emotive words, preferably with some repetition. However, use the wrong words and it will fall flat. How does this sound?

'We will talk and talk and talk once more, to save the Party we are fond of.'

It doesn't work, does it?

4. Use frequent signposts
Give the audience frequent signposts to tell them where you are heading and what is coming next. The following words and phrases all act as signposts:

Firstly   Secondly   Thirdly   And finally   To begin with   However   Nevertheless   On the other hand   In a minute   Later on I will be talking about this in more depth   As I mentioned before...

Audiences feel happy when they have a structure to hold on to. *Tell* them your structure. First you are going to introduce them to a new concept in language teaching, second you will explain how it works, and third you will show them how they can apply it to students in their college.

5. Use the rhetorical question and word YOU
Asking the audience a question will significantly raise their attention level.   The rhetorical question is one of the oldest devices of oratory; it works extremely well as it involves the audience immediately. A rhetorical question is simply one that is floated to the audience without any need for a reply. The idea is simply to get them thinking. Barristers use it all the time.

So how can you use rhetorical questions? Try opening with a question such as. 'How many of you here really know what you want to do when you leave school? Less than half of you, I imagine. Am I right?

Here are some more examples of rhetorical questions from classic speeches.

Example 1

'What are we going to say, comrades? Are we going to accept the defeat? Are we going to say to India, where Socialism has been adopted as the official policy despite all the difficulties facing the Indian community, that the British Labour movement has dropped Socialism here? What are we going to say to the rest of the world? Are we going to send a message from this great Labour movement, which is the father and mother of modern democracy and modern Socialism, that we in Blackpool in 1959 have turned our backs on our principles because of a temporary unpopularity in a temporarily affluent society? (Aneurin Bevan, Labour Party conference, 1959).

This opening paragraph is simply a string of rhetorical questions. Note the use of the word 'comrade' which brings the audience in. (It wouldn't work today.) The speaker's aim is to make the audience feel guilty at their lack of backbone. Also note the use of emotive words (which will be mentioned shortly) like 'father' 'mother' and 'democracy'. It would be very difficult to say 'no' after a speech like that.

Example 2

'You ask what is our policy? I will say: It is to wage war, by sea, land and air, with all our might and with all the strength that God can give us; to wage war against a monstrous tyranny never surpassed in the dark, lamentable catalogue of human crime. That is our policy. You ask, what is our aim. I can answer in one word: it is victory, victory at all cost, victory in spite of all terror, victory, however long and hard the road may be; for without victory there is no survival.' (Winston Churchill's 'Blood, toil, tears and sweat' speech to the House of Commons, May 1940).

The use of the rhetorical question to precede the main statement has the effect of making that statement much stronger. To begin with 'Our policy is to wage war' would be much weaker. See how the Churchill speech also contains examples of repetition and rhythmic construction with frequent use of the word 'victory'.

6. Understand the emotive power of words

We have already seen some illustrations of emotive language. 'Father'
is more emotive that 'Dad' and 'battle' more emotive than 'skirmish'.
Refer back to the extracts from John Wesley and Winston Churchill
and consider the power of the words

drunkenness, gluttony, anger, revenge,
blood, toil, tears and sweat.

Read the text of Martin Luther King's 'I have a dream speech'
(reproduced in full at the end of this chapter), which contains just
about every emotive word you could possibly think of. Look for the
rational argument—there isn't one. The last few paragraphs are
simply a list of geographical features of America with the phrase 'Let
freedom ring' sandwiched between the Rocky Mountains of Colorado and the Alleghenies of Pennsylvania. But as an emotive speech it
worked on that particular audience, helped by Luther King's
powerful, melodic delivery.

Another powerful technique is to speak the language of the
audience, sometimes literally. When President John F. Kennedy
spoke in Berlin at the Berlin Wall he started his speech with the
words: 'Ich bin ein Berliner' (I am a Berliner). Of course, he wasn't—
he was an American. But the effect of those words on the audience
was extremely powerful in making them feel he was on their side.

Consider the sound of the language. Some words have a more
stirring ring to them. For example, the words 'Conservative' and
'Tory' have less of an emotive pull than 'Labour' or 'Democratic'.

Some other strong emotive words often used are

Challenge   Rights   Power   Truth   Strength

And finally, consider the impact of the words in this quotation from
Shakespeare.

'With short, sharp stabs, the multitudinous seas incarnadine.'
Note the mix of monosyllabic Anglo-Saxon English with longer
Latin-based words, and how the sentence has a rhythm.

7. Avoid clichés and redundant language

You can get away with odd clichés like 'Let's bury the hatchet' but, as
a general rule, avoid them. It's better to invent your own metaphor or
simile.

Similes
A simile is a comparison between two things: 'As alike as two peas in a pod' (a cliché).

Metaphors
A metaphor is where one thing is replaced by another. 'It was the court page which bowled me my first Times googly.' (Harold Evans, *Good Times, Bad Times,* 1983).

The first example is a cliché; the second is original. Instead of using a cliché like 'As dead as a Dodo' try something less hackneyed such as 'As dead as a pickled walnut' or 'As inconspicuous as a tarantula on a slice of angel food' (Raymond Chandler)

Original similes and metaphors may also get you a laugh. For some really original and funny similes and metaphors get a video copy of the recent *Blackadder Goes Forth* television series.

Other clichés and overworked phrases to avoid are:

Dead giveaway
Chip off the old block
Butter wouldn't melt in her mouth
Age before beauty
Carrying coals to Newcastle
A foregone conclusion
Second to none
Hook, line and sinker
In full swing
Last but not least
Our lips are sealed
Pure as the driven snow
Start from scratch
The straight and narrow
Through thick and thin
To the bitter end
Too many irons in the fire
Turn over a new leaf
Put your cards on the table
Nothing to write home about

One clever technique is to take a cliché and subtly change a few words. Example: 'As snug as a bug in a rug' becomes 'As safe and snug as a bugger in Rugby' (Dylan Thomas).

On the question of redundant language—that is, language which isn't strictly essential for the meaning, but there for other reasons—

there is redundancy which is necessary (see point 4) and redundancy which grates on the ear—avoid the following

A distance of a hundred yards (cut out 'a distance of')
Rather unique (it is either unique or not)
I myself personally think (cut out 'myself personally')
At this point in time. (Simply say 'Now').

8. Avoid using jargon and abbreviations that people won't understand

In Chapter 3 we mentioned the importance of spelling out abbreviations and acronyms in full. Instead of saying the TGWU say the Transport and General Workers Union, instead of the CPVE say the Certificate of Pre-Vocational Education—unless you are absolutely sure that everyone in the audience understands the terms.

However, there may be other phrases which you regard as common parlance which need to be explained. In *The Complete Plain Words* Sir Ernest Gowers discovered a phrase from a Government circular: 'Distribution of industry policy', a phrase apparently understood in Government Departments but nowhere else.

Probably the worst area for jargon and gobbledy-gook is that of computers. Try and make sense of this extract from a computer manual.

Carrying out a series of copy instructions

When you have a number of files to copy, you won't always be able to find a template that picks out just the files you want. So instead of using one PIP command to copy all the files, you will have to use a number of separate PIP commands. To help you do this, PIP has a special Multiple Command Mode in which it prompts you for the next file to copy.

To start using PIP in Multiple Command Mode, you just type:

P I P

This command loads the PIP utility into memory and starts it running. PIP then prompts you for the details of the copy you want to make by displaying an asterisk on the screen. You then type these details in the form:

destination = source

In other words, what you type is the PIP command for the copy you want to make but without the PIP.

---

9. Use anecdotes, quotations, illustrations and humour

Pumping out points like a machine gun may bore your audience. They are most likely to remember the little stories and touches of humour than the salient points. However, if you can *link* illustrations and anecdotes to your main points they are more likely to remember what you said.

But where do you find these anecdotes? Some people have a memory for jokes and stories: others do not. Fortunately, there are lots of useful books you can refer to, such as *The 637 Best Things Anybody Ever Said* (Robert Byrne) and *The Book of Heroic Failures* (Stephen Pile). See the bibliography at the end of this book for a list of other useful books.

Take the careers talk at a local school. You are talking about JOURNALISM as a career. Your talk is going to get very boring if you simply rattle off the different ways of getting into the profession. However, if you have a good story of how one of the top journalists started by being rejected by a top newspaper as having 'no talent for words' then you can build part of your speech around the story.

A classic story is the one about the author Margaret Mitchell who touted her book *Gone with the Wind* around several publishers. One publisher she visited rejected it for being 'far too long' and 'too risky' because it was set in the Deep South rather than the American West. (See the next chapter for a story-telling exercise based on this.)

A word about telling jokes. Some teachers of presentation skills advise against starting with a joke. Others say that it is acceptable *but only if the joke is relevant.*

If you don't tell jokes well, don't try. Women, on the whole, don't tell a good joke, though of course there are well known exceptions.

See the sections on beginning and ending for more help on anecdotes, illustrations and jokes.

10. Avoid using dry facts and statistics without making meaningful comparisons.

Statements like: 'A silicon chip measures no more than 5mm by 3mm' only comes alive when compared to everyday objects. Say instead: 'A silicon chip, which can process information ten times faster than the human brain, is smaller than your thumbnail.'

General rules when using figures are:

- Use round figures where possible and avoid decimal points or fractions. 'Just over ten per cent' is better than 'ten point one per cent.'

- Words like 'one third' are better than 'thirty-three and a third per cent.'
- Compare height, length and area to people and other things. 'About the length of a wicket' and 'About the size of a football pitch' helps people to visualise.

11. Remember that audience memory is limited

Your audience will probably only remember a tenth of what you have said and most of that will be at the beginning and at the end.

The human memory operates on three levels. First, there is **sensory memory** (lasts a few seconds); second, there is **short term memory** (a few minutes to several days); and third, there is **long term memory** (years, probably permanently). What you should be interested in is how sensory experiences are transferred to short and long term memory.

So what makes people remember?

The brain hears, sees or experiences something—a message. It makes a response—usually an emotional response linked to a need such as survival. The message registers in the brain because it is large, loud, repetitive or because it makes a direct connection with a need. It then passes into short term memory. Not all messages will trigger an emotional response, *but the ones that do will be more likely to be retained.*

- As you write you will need to think like a listener.

Remember in Chapter 3 we looked at how different people process information, either in pictures, sounds or feelings, and occasionally in abstract/verbal form? When you are writing a speech try and get people to visualise a scene, hear sounds or dialogue and feel sensations. Use words which cover all three modes of processing information and sensory experiences.

Example
'Try and picture this scene...' (for visual types)
'Can you hear what I'm trying to say?' (for auditory types)
'Perhaps you get a feeling...' (for kinesthetic types).

Michael Gelb, author of *Present Yourself*, has five keys to audience recall:

1. Begin powerfully and give the audience an overview of what's coming next.

2. Repeat regularly.

3. Emphasise key points by trying to make them unusual.

4. Maximise involvement. Use rhetorical questions and YOU.

5. End powerfully. The audience are more likely to remember your last words.

Checklist
Other tips for helping the audience to concentrate:

- Is your argument easy to follow and the structure clear?

- Have you pitched it at the right level—not too complicated and not too simple? People switch off when they can't remember or when they've heard it all before.

- Have you kept something up your sleeve to surprise the audience? If they know what's coming they won't listen.

- Have you included some unusual stories and words? When presented with a list of words, people will remember the ones which stand out as being unusual and different from the rest.

- Will you keep referring to the audience either through questions or use of the word YOU? Always remember they are *there*!

- Bear in mind that their attention will start to flag after about 20 minutes unless you change your approach or break the pattern.

- Always remember the importance of *emotions*.

In the next chapter we will look at the importance of what you sound like when you speak and how your voice can command attention. This is just as important as *what* you say, perhaps even more so. Then we will look at what you *look* like and how to use visuals effectively.

BEGINNINGS

Probably the hardest place to start is at the beginning. Your opening remarks are crucial if you are to get the audience on your side. People spend hours trying to get those opening phrases exactly right.
    One useful model for opening a speech is AIDA:

Gain *Attention*
Attract *Interest*
Create *Desire* (or Anxiety)
Stimulate *Action*

Example
'Good afternoon ladies and gentlemen. It is rather appropriate that the temperature outside is over 90 degrees Fahrenheit, as global warming is the subject we are going to look at this afternoon.' (Attention). 'By the year 2000, if the present weather predictions come true, the south of England will have the same climate as the South of France and bananas will be growing in Kent.' (Interest).

'Imagine being able to have your annual fête without having to plan for inclement weather or bask on the beach without shivering?' (Desire). 'But would you really like to see the lush green English countryside reduced to parched yellow?' (Anxiety).

'We are going to look at the *real* implications of a dramatic change in our weather patterns and examine what we can do to control its ill-effects.' (Action).

Some possible openings

Jokes
Not to be advised unless you really are a good joke teller. *Never* tell a joke unless it is directly related to what you are going to talk about next. Jokes are to be treated warily.

Hard-hitting statements
These are a good way of arousing attention and making people sit up in their seats. Remember John F. Kennedy's famous opening statement 'Ich bin ein Berliner'.

Statistics can often be useful here. (See the bibliography for suggested books.) However, avoid using too many figures—they soon become meaningless. Don't say: 'Five hundred and forty-seven people died on the roads last month.' It doesn't mean anything unless you compare it to something else—other causes of death, statistics for other countries, for the same month last year, and so on. Say 'one in ten people' rather than 'ten per cent of the population'.

A clear plan of the structure
Tell your audience your purpose and what is coming next. They love signposts and structures. This may not be the most exciting way of opening, but at least it makes your purpose clear. 'Ladies and gentlemen, following some research into computing systems, it's clear that our department needs to speed up our work and increase efficiency. So I am now going to explain the main systems which we could consider purchasing and recommend a system to fit our needs within our budget.'

An appeal
This is most appropriate for fund raising talks where you are asking people to give money. Although the main appeal should be made at the end, your introduction could include the purpose of your speech, which is to persuade people to give generously to a worthy cause. However, if the point is laboured too much, and the benefits not outlined, the appeal could fall flat. It should be *very* brief as an introduction. For example:

'Ladies and gentlemen. Thank you for allowing me to speak to you tonight. I am here on behalf of a charity which raises funds for research into... sclerosis. Like many voluntary associations, we rely heavily upon donations from... I would like to tell you a little about what we are doing, and show where you could be of particular help.'

A rhetorical question
A rhetorical question is one which requires no response. Its purpose is to gain the audience's attention. It makes a good introduction because it immediately draws them into the speech. For example: 'How many of you here tonight have stopped to think what would happen if you lost your job tomorrow?'

A quotation
This is a good way of starting, but only if the quotation is relevant. Take this quotation from Benjamin Disraeli, on becoming Prime Minister in 1868: 'I have climbed to the top of the greasy pole'. That might be an apt introductory statement for a person replying to their appointment to some responsible position. See *The Guide to Political Quotations* (Longman) for some useful quotations.

For more useful quotations – send the end of this chapter. Any book of quotations or books like *Janner's Complete Speechmaker* (Greville Janner MP) or *YOU magazine's book of JOURNOLOGISTS* could also help you.

An anecdote
Starting with a 'folksy tale' was a favourite technique of The Great Communicator, President Ronald Reagan. It is also a nice way to gain the audience's interest before hitting them with your main point. To succeed with anecdotes you need a good sense of timing. If they concerned you personally, they are likely to be more effective.

Opening forms of address
One last point—you may have a set form of address to use before you

launch into your opening statement along the lines of 'Your Royal Highness, my lords, ladies and gentlemen...'. Always check forms of address, who will be present, and that you have got them in the right order, with the most important people mentioned first.

Openings to avoid

- Starting weakly with an apology. *Never* tell them you're nervous or inexperienced.

- Starting with a joke that is irrelevant to the rest of your speech.

- Making a long preamble before getting to the point.

- Telling people that you are going to try and persuade them to do something. Leave the 'commercial' until the end—*suggest* rather than instruct.

- A weak beginning. Always begin with something powerful.

Examples of opening statements

'Over one hundred thousand people die every year by gas.'

'What is the largest killer in this country? It's not heart disease, noɪ cancer, nor alcohol. It's the motor car.'

'A hundred years ago a man died: he died immortal.'(Victor Hugo)

'Did you know that Queen Marie Antoinette and Jayne Mansfield shared identical bust measurements?'

'An old French proverb says: Life is half spent before one knows what life is.'

'Twixt the optimist and the pessimist the difference is droll. The optimist sees the doughnut, whilst the pessimist sees the hole.'

'This is not the first time this week that I have had to get up from a warm seat with a piece of paper in my hand.'

'Back in ancient Greece, Aristotle advised women to eat certain spiders as a contraceptive and men had to pickle their private parts in vinegar. We've come a long way since then.'

ENDINGS

You can use some of the same techniques for ending your speech as you have for the beginning. Anecdotes, jokes (only if directly relevant), hard-hitting statements, quotations and appeals can all work just as well at the end, although you wouldn't necessarily use the same ones. Plans of the structure are obviously only relevant at the beginning.

Here are some other ways of ending a presentation.

Summaries

You can summarise the findings of a survey, or repeat the main points as simply statements. However, try to say something in a different way, rather than repeat word-for-word what you have said before. A three part 'action plan' will work well: people tend to remember things better in that form. If you can make one final point by bringing other main points together then so much the better. 'The whole is greater than the sum of the parts.'

Recommendations and appeals

This is like a call to action. You've made your points and now you want the audience to go away and do something. It's a positive way to end. Appeals are usually all about money or voting. There's not much point in giving a wonderful charity speech extolling the virtues of your organisation and the sterling work it is doing on limited funds without actually asking people for money and telling them what will happen to it.

Food for thought

'In conclusion, I would like you to go away with this thought...'

Endings to avoid

- ending with a long story;
- keeping on telling the audience you've nearly finished and saying things like 'And finally' several times;
- ending with a whimper. 'Well that's about it then...';
- apologising for boring people and keeping them long;
- introducing a new topic.

And finally, always end promptly on time.

Examples of closing statements

'I am too much of a realist to believe that we are going to achieve our purpose in a day. We have only laid the foundations of peace. The superstructure is not even begun.' (Neville Chamberlain).

'So in conclusion, I would like to make three recommendations...'

'And so, I leave you with this final thought. Just stop and think for a moment what would have happened if...'

'So—don't go home and think about it. You have a golden opportunity to change your life. Do it now.'

'And finally, I'd like to summarise the main reasons why your company needs to computerise. It will halve your costs, drastically reduce administration time, and double your output.'

PUTTING YOUR IDEAS TOGETHER—WRITING THE SPEECH

You now have a terrific structure, a mind-blowing introduction and thought-provoking conclusion and your middle section includes some hard-hitting points, backed with solid examples and facts, peppered with illustrations, anecdotes and humour. But do you need the full text in front of you, or will you risk putting down the main points (key words) onto cue cards or a flipchart? Or will you learn your speech and talk impromptu? (not recommended to inexperienced speakers.) Whichever method you choose there are certain points worth bearing in mind if you want to avoid the embarrassment of losing your place, dropping your notes or other cock-ups.

Useful hints when preparing a speech to be read

- Use stiff paper that doesn't rustle.
- Type in double spacing with plenty of margin space for notes and emphases.
- Number each page clearly.
- Use one side of the paper only.
- Don't have a sentence running onto a new page or you will find yourself pausing at the wrong place in mid-sentence while you find the next page.
- If you are using a lectern (try and get hold of one) put two sheets down on the lectern side by side so you don't have to shunt the page you have just read to the back of the script. You can just move it to the left (or right).
- Use coloured pens for marking different sections and indicating where you intend to use audio-visual aids.

Translating written into spoken English
You will probably need to rewrite the whole speech translating it from

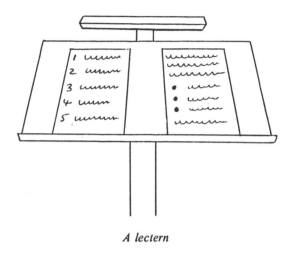

A lectern

essay style into colloquial style, as in the Ovaltine advertisement earlier in this chapter. If you're still not quite clear what it meant by *spoken* English try reading aloud a story from a newspaper. It will probably sound a little long-winded (unless you are reading from a paper like *The Sun*) and not punchy enough for speech. Try rewriting the story as for a TV or radio news bulletin.

Example 1
Take this piece of text:

'Learning a foreign language comes naturally to some people but others find it a real struggle. Why is this? There are several factors which inhibit language learning. The first is simply a lack of confidence. Many of us are just too afraid to speak up in case we make a fool of ourselves. The second reason is lack of motivation. If you don't actually *need* another language, if you can survive with English, then why bother? It's basic laziness. Thirdly, some people have a natural aptitude for languages, women more so than men. The Lebanese, Dutch and Scandinavians often speak several languages fluently. (The Arab races as a whole seem to find languages relatively easy.) And finally, the way people are taught has a bearing on how quickly they pick up a language.'

Now see how this looks on the page when prepared for a spoken presentation:

Example 2

Text	*Visuals*

Learning a foreign <u>language</u>
comes <u>naturally</u> to some people.
But others find it a real <u>struggle</u>.//

Why is this?///

There are several factors which
<u>inhibit</u> language learning.//

The first is simply a lack of
<u>confidence</u>.//   Slide CONFIDENCE
Many of us are just too afraid
to speak up/in case we make a <u>fool</u>
of ourselves.//

The second reason/is lack of <u>motivation</u>./// Slide MOTIVATION

If you don't actually <u>need</u> another language./
If you can survive with English.
Then why bother? It's basic <u>laziness</u>.

Thirdly, some people have a natural   Slide APTITUDE
<u>aptitude</u> for languages,
<u>women</u> more so than *men*.//
The <u>Lebanese</u>, <u>Dutch</u> and Scandinavians
often speak several languages <u>fluently</u>.//
(The Arab races as a whole, incidentally,
seem to find languages relatively easy.)///

And finally, /the way people are
<u>taught</u> has a bearing on how quickly   Slide TEACHING
they pick up a language.///

Note The markings tell the speaker which words to emphasise
(underlining) and where to put pauses (/   //   ///).
   Before transferring a text into this format, try a **timed rehearsal** to
see how long it takes. (In Chapter 10 we see how to rehearse your
speech and prepare yourself.) If you have a 30 minute slot you
shouldn't talk for longer than 32 minutes. We speak at around 150
words a minute but you may be quicker or slower. Time yourself.

Then be prepared to weed out unnecessary material. In *How to Make Effective Business Presentations* author John May recommends that you mark each paragraph in the text as E (Essential), N (Necessary) or D (Desirable). Then you can start cutting the Ds if you have to.

Cue cards

If you are a little unsure about speaking in public then it is better to stick to the script. However, using cue cards will make your speech sound more spontaneous.

Cue cards (sized 6 × 4 ins, 7 × 5 ins or larger) act as memory joggers and are best used for situations like after-dinner speeches. They are not so good for speeches where the language has to be very precise or where statistics are to be used.

When preparing cue cards:

- Number each card clearly.
- Tag them together with a hole in one corner.
- Make sure each card contains one key point.
- Make sure you have written down any key quotations in full or any particular statistics or information you can't rely on your memory for.

Taking the speech on languages, this is how it could appear on a set of cue cards.

Card No. 1.
Language learning – natural
                    – struggle
Why?

Card No. 2.
1. Confidence – fool
2. Motivation – lazy
3. Natural aptitude – Lebanese, Dutch, Scandinavians
4. Teaching methods

Alternatively, points 2, 3 and 4 could be on separate cards.

Prompt devices

These are used by newsreaders. They read from a moving scroll which feeds through a screen directly in their eye line. Two systems are **Autocue** and **Portaprompt**. Some speakers now have a transparent screen in front of them which works in the same way. If presented with a similar device then practise using it beforehand, as your script will move over the screen at a set speed.

Flipcharts and OHP transparencies
Some people like to use their flip charts and OHP transparencies as prompt devices. The only snag is that the speaker sometimes has to turn round or lose eye contact with the audience to read the prompts. When using this method, the speaker should have a spare copy of the visuals in front of him so that he doesn't have to keep on looking at a screen or a flip chart.

Once you have written the basic presentation, then you need to start rehearsing it. You may need some voice coaching (see Chapter 6).

CHECKLIST
— Have you rewritten your speech into spoken English? Does it flow or does it sound stilted?

— Are most of your sentences short (less than 20 words)?

— Are you using mostly simple vocabulary that the audience will easily understand?

— Is your material jargon-free? If not, will every member of the audience understand the jargon?

— Is your sentence construction straightforward? Are you using active, direct speech?

— Have you included some rhetorical questions?

— Look at your choice of words. Do some of them have the right emotional appeal? Do they *sound* good?

— Are you using lots of repetition and rhythmic devices?

— Are you giving the audience signposts so they know where they are in the speech?

— Have you checked for clichés and redundancy?

— Are all your facts accurate and proven? Will you be able to answer some clever-dick correcting you on facts?

— Do your statistics make sense? Are they written as comparisons rather than dry figures?

— Do your jokes and stories fit into the theme of your speech? Are they relevant? Will anyone in the audience be offended by anything?

— Do you have a powerful opening?

— Is your conclusion equally powerful or apt?

— Have you typed out your speech onto paper with double spacing, laid out as suggested?

— If using cue cards, can you speak around the key words without fumbling?

— Have you rehearsed and timed your speech?

Good. Now you are ready to work on your voice and delivery.

Martin Luther King's 'I have a dream' speech (1963)

I have a dream that my four little children will one day live in a nation where they will not be judged by the colour of their skin but by the content of their character.

I have a dream today.

I have a dream that one day the state of Alabama, whose governor's lips are presently dripping with the words of interposition and nullification, will be transformed into a situation where little black boys and black girls will be able to join hands with little white boys and white girls and walk together as sisters and brothers.

I have a dream today.

I have a dream that one day every valley shall be exalted, every hill and mountain shall be made low, the rough places will be made plain, and the crooked places will be made straight, and the glory of the Lord shall be revealed, and all flesh shall see it together.

This is our hope. This is the faith with which I return to the South. With this faith we will be able to hew out of the mountain of despair a stone of hope. With this faith we will be able to work together, to pray together, to struggle together, to go to jail together, to stand up for freedom together, knowing that we will be free one day.

This will be the day when all of God's children will be able to sing with new meaning 'My country 'tis of thee, sweet land of liberty, of thee I sing. Land where my fathers died, land of the pilgrim's pride, from every mountainside, let freedom ring.'

And if America is to be a great nation this must become true. So let freedom ring from the prodigious hilltops of New Hampshire! Let freedom ring from the mighty mountains of New York! Let freedom ring from the heightening Alleghenies of Pennsylvania!

Let freedom ring from the snowcapped Rockies of Colorado!

Let freedom ring from the curvaceous peaks of California!

But not only that; let freedom ring from the Stone Mountain of Georgia!

Let freedom ring from every hill and mole hill of Mississippi. From every mountainside, let freedom ring.

When we let freedom ring, when we let it ring from every village and every hamlet, from every state and every city, we will be able to speed up that day when all of God's children, black men and white men, Jews and Gentiles, Protestants and Catholics, will be able to join hands and sing in the words of that old Negro spiritual, 'Free at last! Free at last! Thank God almighty, we are free at last!'

SOME USEFUL QUOTATIONS & STATISTICS

Statistics

100% of London bankers and stockbrokers believe that ties are a very clear indication of a person's education and background ('The Tie Report' 1987 by Munro & Forster PR for Tie Rack shops).

100% of British men will experience impotence at some time in their lives (Marriage Guidance Council in *Today*, Nov 1987).

99% of live British babies are born in hospital ('Social Trends').

99% of adults in the UK are suffering from gum disease (Wisdom survey/ *Essentials* magazine, Feb 1988).

98% of Britons suffer from tooth decay. (*Daily Mail*, Jan 1988).

95% of British brides say they made love with their fiancés before their wedding day. (*Wedding and Home*, 1987).

90% of British people feel that waste from nuclear electricity stations has a serious effect on the environment. (British Social Attitudes/Social and Community Planning Research, 1987).

80% of British women read horoscopes. (*The Independent*, Jan 1988).

70% of British consumers say that if a service is particularly good, they wouldn't mind too much if the goods were a little more expensive. (*Are you being served*/Leo Burnett Nov 1987).

60% of Britons agree that TV violence gives children the impression that murder occurs daily. (IBA/*The Times*, Jan 1988).

55% of British men sleep in the nude. (*Women's World* magazine, 1987).

50% of Britain's unemployed smoke. (Institute for Fiscal Studies/*Today*, 1987.

40% of British holidaymakers now venture out of their hotels to eat out in restaurants. (*The Guardian*, Jan 1988).

Americans have a 960% better chance of dying from choking on food at home than being killed by a terrorist abroad.

More than 11 people die every hour from causes that are directly attributable to smoking.

Fifteen people in the UK die of cancer every hour.

In the UK we eat about 80,000 kilograms of sweets an hour making us the biggest sweet eaters in the world.

In the UK we spend more than £1,500,000 every hour of every day on alcoholic drinks.

Quotations

Some are born greater, some achieve greatness, and some have greatness thrust upon 'em. (Malvolio in Shakespeare's *Twelfth Night*, Act 2).

Some are born great, some achieve greatness, and some hire public relations officers. (Daniel Boorstin, American educator and writer).

Management is the art of getting other people to do all the work. (Anon).

If you can keep your head when all about you are losing theirs, it's possible you haven't grasped the situation. (Jean Kerr, American essayist and playwright).

I have climbed to the top of the greasy pole. (Benjamin Disraeli on becoming Prime Minister, 1868).

I don't mind how much my ministers talk — as long as they do what I say. (Margaret Thatcher, 1980).

One man's wage increase is another man's price increase. (Harold Wilson).

To be without some of the things you want is an indispensable part of happiness. (Bertrand Russell, philosopher).

It is always the best policy to speak the truth, unless of course you are an exceptionally good liar. (Jerome K. Jerome in *The Idler*).

Sources

The Pan/Chambers book of Business Quotations (Pan).
The 637 best things anybody ever said by Robert Burne (Sphere).
Contradictory Quotations (Longman).
100% British by Jo Eastwood (Penguin).
The Book of British Trivia by Jim and Peggy Converse (Javelin).

6
Finding a Voice

You have written your speech and it reads well. Your subject matter is right for the audience. Your words are carefully chosen. Your speech is well structured with lots of anecdotes and lively examples.

You are ready to try reading it out loud in private. You open your mouth and somehow it just doesn't sound right. You're just not happy with your voice—it sounds dull, stilted and monotonous.

There have been so many speakers, including captains of industry, who have written papers full of interesting research and pithy statements, only to deliver them in a tone of voice that resembles the droning of an antique bagpipe. No wonder there is such a demand for professional presentation courses. At worst, a poor presentation can cost a company an important deal and a lot of money. It's rarely *what* is said that's at fault, rather it's how it comes across.

It is so easy to murder the most poetic prose and vibrant verse by making it sound excruciatingly dull—it really doesn't take much effort. In *The Secrets of Successful Speaking and Business Presentations* by Gordon Bell, a certain unfortunate Financial Director of a large company is cited. He knew everything there was to know about the finances of the company, but when it came to putting them across to an audience he was totally wooden. 'The deathwatch beetle had got into him', says Mr Bell, using an apt metaphor. 'As an inflictor of pain he made Torquemada look like a novice.' The audience of Royals and Sheiks and their entourages apparently departed after 20 minutes of his speech leaving only a few faithfuls to witness the dying embers of the verbal torture. The outcome was that the company lost a contract worth £184 million and thousands of people lost their jobs. The Finance Director was persuaded to retire.

The problem is that we don't necessarily sound to others the way we sound to ourselves. Only when we hear ourselves recorded on tape or

84

video can we really appreciate that we are mumbling or using too many 'ums' and 'ers'. The way you sound can be changed if you are prepared to work at it. Using a voice coach will help enormously but you will obviously have to pay for one. Professional voice coaches have helped people 'lose' their accents within a few months and transformed dull voices into ones that hold people's attention. The key to changing your voice is learning to breathe properly and spending time on specific vocal exercises. (More on this later.)

Common delivery problems
The most common problems with delivery are:

1. Making the text sound *read* rather than *said.*
2. Insufficient use of *pauses.*
3. Speaking too *fast*—rushed delivery.
4. Speaking too *softly* and not *projecting* the voice.
5. Too high a *pitch*—often due to nerves. (Women are apt to suffer from this more than men.)
6. Lack of *clarity.* Indistinct and muffled speech.
7. Problems with *tone*—lack of resonance, speaking through the nose, hoarseness.
8. Lack of proper *intonation.* Equal *emphasis* on words.
9. Speech *appendages.* Irritating words such as 'ums', 'ers', 'sort of' and 'like'.

Other speech variations which people sometimes wish to change or get rid of include stammering, lisping, accents and problems with certain sounds (like 'r's' which come out as 'w's'). However, no one should be encouraged to modify their speech patterns unless they really need to. Regional accents for example can be very attractive. Stammering is a different matter and it is not within the scope of this book to deal with speech impediments as such, although there are excellent speakers who manage despite their stammer.

The important point is that none of these 'problems' should be seen in isolation. There are circumstances where a speech problem can be turned to an advantage by making it distinctive (as with TV presenter Jonathan Ross's difficulty with 'r's' and singer/actress Toyah Wilcox's lisp). The most important vocal skill you need to master is *variety.* If you can make your voice both high and low, slow and fast, soft and loud within one sentence, then you are beginning to master vocal fluency. You don't have to sound like a Welsh tenor or make your voice do acrobatics: subtle inflections can be just as effective.

Without a tape recorder, it is difficult to demonstrate the different between a voice that makes the text come alive and one which leaves the listener in a state of near slumber or total boredom. Why not listen to recordings of some of the great actors such as Laurence Olivier or Peggy Ashcroft reading the Bible or Shakespeare? How about listening to broadcasters such as Brian Redhead (for speaking straight to the point), Ned Sherrin (fast, pacey delivery which keeps you on your toes), Anna Ford (well-rounded vowels and a voice that is easy on the ear), or your favourite radio DJ? Try reading one of the news bulletins or the television script at the end of this chapter and you'll understand that broadcasting isn't as easy as it sounds. However, there is a knack to it, which can be taught and developed.

Actor and voice coach Terry Besson has trained actors at the Royal Academy of Dramatic Arts and coached Dustin Hoffman for his role as Shylock in *The Merchant of Venice*. He says the worst thing you can do is to try and isolate one particular problem, such as a lisp, and try and correct it. The voice has a number of elements which are all interlinked. To improve vocal quality you need to work on *everything*—breathing, intonation, projection and resonance.

BREATHING AND RELAXATION

Correct breathing is the key to good vocal delivery. Terry Besson says that if you can't get your breathing right then nothing else will go right. He spends the first two sessions with his pupils focusing on posture and teaching them to breathe from the diaphragm.

Exercise: breathing from the diaphragm
Start by lying down on the floor with your head supported on a cushion. Put your hands just under your rib cage on the diaphragm so that the finger tips are just touching. Take in a deep breath and push the rib cage out. You should feel the muscles of the diaphragm, and your finger tips should part slightly. If they don't you are not doing the exercise right. Exhale and breathe in again.Then try holding your breath for 10 seconds, 15 seconds and finally for 20 seconds. Breathing techniques as used in yoga are very useful here but yoga teachers recommend that you go to classes rather than use a book.

Exercise: preliminary relaxation
Once you feel you have mastered diaphragmatic breathing then try the same exercise standing up. If your posture is hunched or you throw

your head back then your breathing will be constricted and you may need to do some preliminary relaxation exercises. Try these.

Clench your hands and then release them. Do the same with your shoulders (hunch them and then release), your leg muscles, your arms, your feet and finally scrunch up your face and then release. Now try the deep breathing exercises again, standing up. Make sure that you don't hunch your shoulders—get a friend to put their hands on your shoulders to stop them moving up.

Here are some more relaxation exercises:

- Roll the head around from left to right and right to left. Let it drop. Then roll it round clockwise and anti-clockwise.
- Hunch the shoulders up again—and release.
- Become a string puppet. Put your hands up on the air as if there were strings on them. Stretch as far as you can go. Then let them drop by your side.
- Shake your hands one at a time.

The Alexander Technique
This is used by a lot of actors as a way of improving their breathing and voice quality. It was originated by an Australian actor F. Matthias Alexander (1869-1955) who suffered from stress and loss of voice during performances. What he discovered, through looking at himself in the mirror, was that before a performance he would start to tense his neck muscles, throw back his head, shorten his height and breathe erratically. The technique, which is based on correcting bodily posture, is now taught all over the world. It has become recognised as one of the best ways of aligning posture with breathing in order to produce the quality of the voice and get rid of nerves.

Note The technique cannot be learned from a book and must be taught. For a list of recognised teachers contact The Society of Teachers of the Alexander Technique, 10 London House, 206 Fulham Road, London SW10 9EL. Tel: (071) 351 0828.

Try reciting this passage on one breath.

Do breath tests test the breath?
Yes, that's the best of a breath test,
and the best test of the best breath is
that the best breath stands the breath test.

VOCAL EXERCISES

Once you feel comfortable about your breathing then you can start working on vocal exercises, starting with vowel sounds. The object of the exercises is to give your voice more variety, clarity and resonance. If you want to alter your accent then you will need to work on specific vowel sounds and examine the way your shape your mouth.

Vowel sounds

Humming exercises are good warm-ups. Try this one. Put your hand on top of your head and start to hum on one note. You should feel a tingle in your lips and some resonance on the top of your head. Singers start with exercises like this.

Try humming an octave going up and down the scale. (If you can't sing properly don't worry—just have a go.) Now try singing the following vowel sounds with the prefix M staying on one note with one continuous sound. If you need to (and you probably will) take a breath after Mo.

Me May Mar Mo Moo Mer My More

Getting well-rounded vowel sounds means opening the throat. Nasal vowels often result from constrictions in the throat due to incorrect breathing, a half-closed mouth or throwing the head back too much. Another problem is not opening the mouth wide enough—a particular problem of the English aristocracy. Next time you meet an aristocrat or Sloane Ranger (assuming you don't every day!) watch how the mouth moves—it basically doesn't. The actor Edward Fox (*The Go Between, The Day of the Jackal*) is very good at speaking in the characteristic clipped accent—watch how little he moves his mouth.

Two useful exercises to open up the throat are yawning, and waggling the jaw. Start by giving a really good yawn. Then open your mouth as wide as you can and waggle your jaw from side to side. Try and make your mouth as mobile as you can—like rubber. This exercise is also very good for general articulation.

Now try talking in your poshest voice whilst keeping your mouth and jaw as immobile as possible. The word 'house' may come out as 'hice'. (The British don't have a 'stiff upper lip' for nothing—it actually helps them pronounce those aristocratic clipped vowels.) Say 'The water in Majorca doesn't taste like what it ought to' in your best Sloane Ranger clipped accent, taking care to pronounce the 'j' in Majorca as 'y'. Now say: 'The water in Majorca don't taste like what it ought'a' taking care to pronounce the 'j' this time. It should sound like 'The wor'a in Merjorca down taist loik wo i or'a'.

The point is that to recite the second speech with the right Cockney accent you must adopt a totally different mouth position with more mobility. So if you want to change your accent to develop more flexibility with your voice you should be able to shape your mouth in different ways. An interesting exercise is to watch TV with the sound turned off and try to guess the kind of accent people have.

Additional vowel exercises
Here are some more vowel exercises....

1. Who Would Know Aught Of Art Must Learn And Then Take His Ease

2. Hoot Hook Hoe Hawk Hock Hard Hut Heard Had Head Hay Hid Heed

3. Say this nursery rhyme opening your mouth as wide as you can:

> Ba ba black sheep, have you any wool?
> Yes sir, please sir, three bags full.
> One for the master and one for the dame,
> And one for the little boy who lives down the lane.

Articulation

Clarity in the voice means pronouncing each syllable without mumbling or 'swallowing' vowels. The jaw waggling exercises are very useful here.

Most of us fail to pronounce certain vowels in sentences. Say the word 'peat' on its own. Now say the words 'peat bog'. You probably lost the 't' somewhere and said something like 'pea bog' with a short 'e' sound.

Say these words aloud:

SANDWICH POSTMAN

The words probably sounded more like

SAMWICH and POSMAN.

Say them again pronouncing the D in SANDWICH and the T in POSTMAN.

Exercises: tongue twisters

> Peter Piper picked a peck of pickled pepper
> Where's the peck of pickled pepper
> Peter Piper picked? (P)

Around the ragged rocks the ragged rascal ran (R).

Ten ton Tessie from Tennessee (T).

She sells sea shells on the sea shore (S).

I am the very model of a modern Major General (M).

If you find these difficult, go back to basics with exercises like these. Make sure you keep up the rhythm.

(P)   ppp-ppp-ppp-pee
ppp-ppp-ppp-poo
ppp-ppp-ppp-paw
ppp-ppp-ppp-pah
ppp-ppp-ppp-pay

Repeat this exercise for other consonants like T, K, F, S, B, D, V, Z, Ch and Dr. With the L sound do the exercise twice, once with the tongue outside the mouth and once with the tongue inside.

Exercises for tongue control

Precise articulation means placing the tongue very carefully. Try saying the word 'trip' whilst putting your tongue flat against the roof of your mouth or pulling it back—it's almost impossible. Now try saying it with the tip of the tongue against the hard palette behind your teeth on the roof of the mouth and you should find it much easier.

Some tricky sounds include 'ng' and 'ts'. Here are some exercises for these:

Moong	Mohng	Mawng	Mahng	Merng	Mayng	Meeng
Tsoo	Tsoh	Tsaw	Tsah	Tser	Tsay	Tsee

Try this exercise which is good both for vowel sounds and for consonants:

To sit in solemn silence in a dull dark dock
In a pestilential prison with a life long lock
Awaiting the sensation of a short sharp shock
From a cheap and chirpy chopper on a big black block.

Trippingly on the tongue

This passage from Shakespeare's *Hamlet* (Act III) will really test your skills of articulation.

Speak the speech, I pray you, as I pronounc'd it to you,
trippingly on the tongue;
but if you mouth it, as many of our players do,
I had as lief the town-crier spoke my lines.
Nor do not saw the air too much with your hand, thus,
but use all gently: for in the very torrent, tempest,
and, as I may say whirlwind of your passion,
you must acquire and beget a temperance that may give it smoothness.
O, it offends me to the soul
to hear a robustious periwig-pated fellow
tear a passion to tatters, to very rags,
to split the ears of the groundlings,
who, for the most part, are capable of nothing
but inexplicable dumb shows and noise.
I would have such a fellow whipped for o'er doing Termagant,
it out-herods Herod. Pray you avoid it.

Finally, here are some tricky phrases that require very precise articulation. If they present real difficulties then consider rewriting them to avoid getting tongue-tied.

A shortage of statistics
Transactional analysis
Cost structures
Management changes
Perennial prerequisites

Speed and rhythm
Speaking with a 'machine gun' delivery, placing an equal emphasis on each word, sounds very monotonous. The English language, unlike the Indian and Latin-based languages, does not place equal emphasis on each syllable.
Read these two sentences aloud:

John comes from Kent.
Jonathan's place of origin is Lancashire.

How long did you take to say each sentence? More-or-less the same, with the second one taking just a little longer? The first sentence has four syllables, whilst the second has twelve, yet you probably spoke each word in the second sentence much more quickly than the words in the first, with the emphasis on Jonathan, origin and Lancashire.
One of the problems people have with reading scripts is that they

frequently lapse into 'machine-gun' delivery and lose the natural rise and fall of the voice. (Listen to Returning Officers reading results at a General Election.) Part of the problem is unfamiliarity with the text: when people are reading rather than speaking, they fail to look far enough ahead in the text and so give each word an equal amount of time, which makes it sound stilted. Marking up a script underlining the words you want to emphasise helps prevent this.

Projection and volume

Being able to project your voice to the back of a room comes with mastery of correct breathing and self-confidence. Normally, people need to project their voice much more than they think, and exaggerate. The problem is that most people have never been in situations where they have to talk to large groups of people before and they are afraid of raising their voice. Practising alone in a room is the best way to start. Take a deep breath into the diaphragm and try 'sending' your voice to three different places—the other side of the room, the next room, the next floor. Try the exercise using this passage from Shakespeare's *Julius Caesar*.

> Friends, Romans, countrymen, lend me your ears.
> I come to bury Caesar, not to praise him.

Say it softly in a whisper, to begin with. Then speak as if addressing an audience of about 20 people. Finally, imagine a hall full of hundreds—try and fill the imaginary hall with your voice. (Wait until you have an empty house and try shouting.)

Pitch

Many voices start getting squeaky as a result of nerves. The throat gets constricted, the head goes back and the voice comes out with a thin reedy sound.

Practise the breathing exercises recommended at the beginning of this chapter and consciously try to bring your voice down. It won't deepen in pitch immediately, but after a few months you may find it is a tone lower.

Do you know how Margaret Thatcher used to speak about 15 years ago? If so you will realise that her voice since came down several tones and became slightly husky. She had voice coaching to make her sound more authoritative and less like a 'posh Tory lady'.

Exercise: lowering your pitch
Try saying these three sentences concentrating on bringing authority

into your voice. Avoid sounding apologetic and consciously try to lower the pitch.

I want you to listen very carefully to what I am saying.
Under no circumstances are you to go into that room.
You will do exactly what I tell you to.

Now try saying this passage, varying the pitch of your voice. Don't force your voice: the change should be subtle.

Higher and higher until it reached the very top.
Down, down, down into the depths.
Lower and lower until it reached the very bottom.
And then up.

Tone

Monotonous voices have very little variety of pitch, speed and volume and use very few pauses. To give your voice variety you need to master the art of inflexion—making your voice go up or down to convey meaning. For instance, when we ask a question, the voice goes up at the end of a sentence. Say the following sentence (a) as a statement, and (b) as a question.

You're going to France this year!
You're going to France this year?

Exercise: no!?
Try saying the word NO in different ways to convey each meaning simply by changing the intonation.

NO (meaning definitely not)
NO (meaning maybe YES)
NO (meaning I'm afraid)
NO (meaning you naughty person)
NO (meaning I don't believe it)
NO (meaning I am angry)
NO (meaning I am really surprised)
NO (meaning YES!)

Exercise: extracting the meat

Now say the following words trying to get as much 'meat' out of them as possible. Draw out the vowels and over-articulate the consonants. Make as much as you can of each word. (Some you may recognise them from Rowan Atkinson's schoolmaster character in *The Secret Policeman's Ball.*)

Blob
Blaire
Higginbottom
Pringle
Plectrum
Dollop
Mole
Mollusc
Undermanager
Splot

Exercise: varying volume, pitch, speed and intonation
Here is another exercise designed to encourage you to vary volume, pitch, speed and intonation. And don't forget to make maximum use of pauses.

'He crept into the room cautiously, looked around and took in every detail. The furniture was thick with dust. An eerie silence pervaded the atmosphere. On the far wall was an image of a woman with black hair and a ghostly white pallor. His heart began to beat faster, faster and still faster. He felt his legs begin to move towards the stairs. Suddenly he found himself running down the oak staircase and then he felt his legs beginning to give way. He tumbled down and down and down to the hall below. Where was he? In a state of semi-consciousness, his head spinning, he heard the distinct sound of a loud gong—clang clang clang, echoing throughout the house—until the silence returned once more.'

Reading children's stories is an excellent way of developing your vocal range and injecting vitality into your speech. In the next Chapter you will find a passage from *Lord of the Rings.* Try reading it aloud.

Tips for making text sound *said* not *read*

Exercise: speaking Shakespeare in modern English
Take the speech from Hamlet on page 91: 'Speak the speech, I pray you, as I pronounced it to you, trippingly on the tongue...'
Imagine you are advising a group of drama students on how to deliver a speech without sounding like a ham actor. You will need to

translate the language of Shakespeare into modern English and *tell* them rather than recite. This is a drama lesson, not a Shakespearian speech.

For example: 'when you do this speech, make it sound as if it trips off the tongue. Don't make it sound like the town crier and don't wave your arms around like this. Be gentle. If you get carried away with passion make your voice sound smooth. It really offends my ear to hear a...'

Exercise: telling the story of Margaret Mitchell
Here is a well known story about the author Margaret Mitchell on her first attempt to find a publisher for *Gone with the Wind*. Read it through first and then try *telling* the story. The secret is to emphasise certain words only and vary the speed.

Back in the 'thirties a young woman walked into a publishing agent's office in New York City with a manuscript of over a thousand pages in her hands. The agent whistled when she laid it on his desk and said:

'It's too long. Who in the world is going to wade through all of that? Can you shorten it?'

'I suppose I could,' the woman replied disconsolately.

'I presume this is your first novel.' the agent said.

She answered: 'Yes, it is.'

The agent asked: 'Have you ever published anything before?'

'No.'

'What is the story about?'

'A young woman living in the South during the Civil War.'

'Too bad you didn't locate it in the West; westerns are very popular right now. What do you call your book?'

'Gone with the Wind.'

'Publishers won't touch it. It's too big a risk. A book by an unknown author would have to be another American tragedy to make a profit... I'll give you the name of a friend of mine who may handle it for you. He has sold a few historical novels, but first I'd strongly recommend that you chop it in half—it's too long.'

Vocal techniques with Lewis Carroll

Here is the poem *Jabberwocky* from Lewis Carroll's *Alice through the Looking Glass*. Of course, it's a nonsense poem, but try and convey the meaning using all the vocal techniques discussed in this chapter—variety of rhythm, speed, volume, pitch and tone:

> 'Twas brillig, and the slithy toves
>   Did gyre and gimble in the wabe:
> All mimsy were the borogroves,
>   And the mome raths outgrabe.
>
> Beware the Jabberwock, my son!
>   The jaws that bite, the claws that catch
> Beware the Jubjub bird, and shun
>   The frumious Bandersnatch!
>
> He took his vorpal sword in hand:
>   Long time the manxome foe he sought—
> So rested he by the Tumtum tree,
>   And stood awhile in thought.
>
> And, as in uffish thought he stood,
>   The Jabberwock, with eyes of flame,
> Came whiffling through the tulgey wood,
>   And burbled as it came.
>
> One, two! One, two! And through and through
>   The vorpal blade went snicker-snack!
> He left it dead and with its head
>   He went galumphing back.

In the next chapter we will explore non-verbal communication and see how body language can add impact. Once you are familiar with the language try reading it through adding gestures—verse three for example lends itself to magnificent sweeping gestures.

Exercise: the meaning of a Shakespearian sonnet
Here is a different passage for practice—one of Shakespeare's sonnets. The temptation is to read it like a party piece at school. Think yourself into the *meaning* of the piece; read it as if the writer of the sonnet is you. The natural rhythm of this piece should help in your reading. Line 6 may present a few problems, as it is essentially a list of parts of the body. Vary the tone on each word to avoid sounding monotonous.

When in the chronicle of wasted time
I see descriptions of the fairest wights,
And beauty making beautiful old rime
In praise of ladies dead and lovely knights,
Then in the blazon of sweet beauty's best,
Of hand, of foot, of lip, of eye, of brow,
I see their antique pen would have exprest
Even such a beauty as you master now.
So all their praises are but prophecies
Of this our time, all your prefiguring;
And for they look'd but with divining eyes,
They had not skill enough your worth to sing:
For we, which now behold these present days,
Have eyes to wonder, but lack tongues to praise.

The next passage from *The Rhyme of the Ancient Mariner* by Samuel Taylor Coleridge is excellent for articulating vowel sounds. Keeping the rhythm of the poetry, try and use your voice to convey emptiness and desolation.

The fair breeze blew, the white foam flew,
The furrow follow'd free;
We were the first that ever burst
Into that silent sea.

Down dropt the breeze, the sails dropt down,
'Twas sad as sad could be;
And we did speak only to break
The silence of the sea!

All in a hot and copper sky,
The bloody Sun, at noon
Right up above the mast did stand,
No bigger than the Moon.

Day after day, day after day,
We stuck, nor breath nor motion;
As idle as a painted ship
Upon a painted ocean.

Water, water, everywhere,
And all the boards did shrink;
Water, water, everywhere,
Nor any drop to drink.

Try and make the words 'day after day' sound heavy (verse 4) and make the most of the alliteration of the 'p' in 'painted' and 'ship'.

Tape record yourself reading these passages and try to identify the aspects of your voice you want to change. If your vowels are sounding flat and the word 'day' sound more like 'die' then you will need to practise the vowel exercises suggested earlier. You may never be asked to stand up and recite poetry, but these exercises are very good practice.

Exercise: reading from radio scripts
Try reading these two sample (fictional) radio scripts based on the style of BBC Radio news bulletins. The secret is to make them sound as if you are speaking to a person in the same room, not reading a script. Read each one through first, then put it aside and *tell* an imaginary friend what the news is all about. Then go back and read it again:

> The Government last night voted for an extra day's official holiday in honour of the black activist Wilson Mobella. The resolution was hotly contested and narrowly avoided defeat by only one vote. Granting a public holiday in the name of someone who is a highly controversial figure is a decision with obvious political significance. The holiday will fall on 23rd July—Mr Mobella's birthday.

> On the eve of national reconciliation talks in Licaragua heavy fighting last night and this morning has increased fears that the talks might have to be postponed. The venue for the talks is supposed to be Panagua airport but the Lydian backed opposition has already said that they won't attend because security at the airport isn't good enough. Colin Payne in Panagua has been telling me whether the talks are in danger of breaking down.

Exercise: reading from a television script
Now try reading this TV script from one of Channel Four's *On Course* programmes produced for the Open College. You may need to practise several times before you get the knack of *talking to the audience* rather than reading the script. Get a friend to listen to you and try and talk *to* them. The margins would be narrower here as the presenter would normally read the script off Autocue, a device where a scroll of paper is fed through a TV monitor so the presenter can read whilst appearing to look straight into the camera.

Hello, and welcome to *On Course*. We're part of the new Open College and this programme is aimed at the people who *do* the training rather than those who receive it.

That means anyone from tutors to receptionists to regional managers—people who need to know about the college and about open learning (we'll explain what that means in a moment). So that even if you have no connection with the Open College this is still the programme for you. Over the next year we'll aim to cover training in the broadest sense.

As the series unfolds it will become clear how Open College trainers differ from the conventional teacher. So *On Course* will demonstrate the skills you need to be a better trainer and look at the courses you need them for; we'll pass on the experience of other trainers around the country; we'll show good practice and ring warning bells about possible pitfalls.

We've installed a brand new switchboard here at Channel Four, so you can be just as much part of the programme as people here in the studio. Ring 01 436 4771 to tell us what *you* think. (We'll ring you back so you don't have to hang on paying for the call.)

Today, Sheila Innes, the Chief Executive of the Open College is under our spotlight and if you have any comments or questions for her, ring us now.

We'll be opening up our 'toolkit' of skills which make a better trainer. How can you make a good 'first impression' in that all-important initial meeting with would-be learners.

Anita Roddick from the Bodyshop will open our casebook, telling us how open learning has helped her firm, and we'll be looking at a perennial training problem at the Business End through the eyes of Sir Richard O'Brien. To take part in the programme ring us now.

THE DISTANCE BETWEEN THE MASTER AND PRESENTER UNITS IS UNLIMITED

How the autocue system works

7
Body Language and Non-Verbal Communication

One of the most surprising findings of research into the way people receive communication messages is that the *visual* impact of communication is more powerful than the verbal.

The much quoted research by Professor Albert Mehrabian has shown that 55% of the impact of a speaker on the audience is visual, 38% of the impact comes from the sound of the voice, and a tiny 7% comes from the content of the words alone. In other words, 'It ain't what you say', nor is it even 'the way that you say it'—it's what you *look* like that counts. You may be wondering why we have just devoted six chapters to the content and to verbal presentation skills. If one were to take the findings of this research literally, then all one need do is wear the right clothes, get star quality grooming, perhaps a face lift, stand up on stage—and talk garbage.

Two very important points are worth making here. Firstly, the research was done in America, where people take more notice of how people look than how they sound. In Britain, where we have a strong literary tradition, verbal skills would probably rate higher in similar experiments. Secondly, the impact of visual communication cannot be separated from sound and content. The different channels are interdependent. However, the visual side of communication *is* important. Remember these three important points:

1. People tend to *believe* what they see rather than what they hear. If you look confident people will believe what you say. If your body language is not congruent (doesn't match) with what you are saying, people will take more notice of what you look like.

2. People often *remember* more of what they see than what they hear. By using visuals and looking good you will reinforce your message and people will remember it. Some people respond much more readily to visual messages than to verbal ones.

3. People are often distracted by visual signals. Speakers are often unaware of how they look, and of the signals they are sending by their own body language. These signals are subtle but very powerful. Irritating mannerisms can totally distract an audience from what you are trying to say.

How we communicate visually

We communicate visually in the following ways:

- through body language, the face and the eyes;
- through what we hear and general physical appearance;
- by using space and proximity;
- through symbols, signs, images and objects;
- through words on paper (or transparencies).

In this chapter we will be looking at
body language
clothes and physical appearance.

In the next chapter we will be looking at
space and proximity
audio-visual aids.

Body language types

First, let's look at certain types of speakers who can be distinguished by their distinct body language.

Peter the prowler

He paces up and down like a lion in a cage. Just as he reaches the edge of the platform he does a swift about turn and paces back again. People at the front of the audience follow his movements like a tennis match. Nobody listens to what he is saying because they are waiting for him to do his little spin and prowl back again.

Olivia the ostrich

She buries her head in her speech which is written out word for word on sheets of paper. Her eyes are locked in a downward arc; she never actually looks at the audience who are all starting to fidget. A pity, because what she has to say is quite interesting.

Johnnie the juggler

He is a wizard with coins, pens, chalk, in fact anything he can throw up in the air. He doesn't know what to do with this hands and so he starts his juggling sequence. Everyone is transfixed waiting for him to drop something. He thinks they are all absorbed in what he is saying, but their minds are elsewhere.

Brenda the bird
She can't keep her hands (wings) still, either. Unfortunately, she doesn't do anything really definite with her hands—they just flap around like a bird. One particular gesture is the semi-circular motion with a bent wrist, characteristic of birds with broken wings trying to take off. Most irritating.

Charlie the chopper
Now he knows what to do with his hands. They are never still— waving around, up and down as if he is handling a meat cleaver or conducting an orchestra with a baton. Arthur Scargill is a master of this chopping motion. The only trouble is how to get the chopping motion synchronised with the speech. If it comes a fraction after the crucial word, which is usually 'struggle' or 'cut', then it looks forced.

Karen the kangaroo
She is perpetually hopping from one foot to the other, springing up and down on her heels, which are too high. Bounce, bounce she goes. Everyone is looking at her legs, seeing exactly what she *does*, and paying no attention to what she *says*.

Norman the nudist
Norman doesn't know what to do with his hands, so he clasps them in front just over his private parts and bends his knees slightly. He looks like a man who been caught with his trousers down. The general impression he gives is rather wimpish and lacking any authority. He doesn't look very relaxed, and nor does his audience.

Larry the leaning tower
Larry feels naked without a lectern because he has to lean on it— usually on one foot. The upper half of his body is draped over the top part of the lectern, possibly because he is unable to stand up without support due to excessive alcohol. Academics favour this position, particularly as it helps them remain upright after a heavy drinks session.

Stella the stork
She loves standing on one leg or twisting her legs around each other until they resemble a plaited loaf. For some unknown reason,

standing on two legs is a problem. The audience is soon transfixed by the contortions of her legs.

BODILY COMMUNICATION

Now let's look at the various elements involved in how you communicate through your body. The body is a very powerful medium of communication. People pick up all kinds of signals for example about the speaker's state of mind, sincerity and confidence. We tend to believe what the body says to us more than what words say to us. Take the stereotype of the sharp second-hand car salesman who tells us that his product is absolutely one hundred per cent genuine and roadworthy 'with one careful owner' but who's face and body language tells you otherwise. What do you believe—the words or your gut reaction to his body language?

Eye contact

Probably the worst thing you can do apart from mumbling inaudibly is not to look at the audience. The first point of contact you have with the audience is through the eyes. Try walking into a room. Turn and face the audience and take a slow look at all the faces; if you find this difficult, fix your gaze on their foreheads. (They will never know). If your audience are facing you in a horseshoe make sure that you turn and look at the two people on the extremities of the horseshoe before you start speaking and then remember to look at them several times during the session. If you are reading your script, make sure you pause and look at the audience from time to time. If their attention is starting to wander they will soon wake up and listen if they sense you are looking at them.

If you avoid eye contact it looks as if you are unsure of yourself or that you don't believe in what you are saying. A broad sweep is better than jerky eye movements with your eyes flitting all over the place—that unsettles them. Don't stare at one person and try and keep each gaze for about three seconds, but no more.

In the days before Autocue, when TV newsreaders had to keep on looking down at their scripts, the effect on the audience of their eyes moving up and down was to make them look shifty. An article about newsreaders appeared in a newspaper with the headline 'Who are the guilty men?', which was rather unfortunate. Bear this in mind when you are reading a script. If you don't look at the audience enough they may mistrust you; if you keep on looking up and down this will have a similar effect. It is better to read a bit and then pause to look up before continuing.

Facial expression

There is nothing more captivating than a smile. When you first walk
into a room look at the audience and smile. This will help you to relax
and make a positive communication. Write the word SMILE onto
your script or draw a little picture to remind you. The message it
conveys to the audience is this: 'I am pleased to be here and looking
forward to meeting you.' This makes the audience feel good and their
mood is conveyed back to you—which helps you feel good, too.

Gestures

Gestures are an integral part of expression through speech, but not
everyone uses them. Generally, they have the following uses:

- They can **illustrate** something—usually the shape or size of an
  object. Try describing the shape of a teapot to someone who has
  never seen one before without using your hands—it's not easy!

- They **emphasise** certain points. The 'baton' gesture, which is like
  a conductor using a baton, used a lot by Arthur Scargill, is
  effective to emphasise key words. The expansive gesture with
  arms sweeping everywhere can be used to emphasise vastness.
  And the gesture with finger and thumb pinched together in an O
  emphasises precision. A word of warning—this gesture has
  different meanings around the world (some of them insulting!).
  Another familiar gesture is the bunch of bananas—open palm
  with finger pointing upwards—which doesn't mean anything in
  particular but seems to be a favourite of academics. Perhaps it
  suggests 'grasping a concept'.

- They convey **specific meanings**. Examples are the hitchhikers'
  sign of the upturned thumb (a rude gesture in the Middle East
  and parts of the Mediterranean) and the farewell wave.
  Generally, these gestures are used without words.

- They indicate the **state of mind** of the speaker. These gestures are
  usually unconscious. The person who has an irritating hand
  gesture which serves no useful purpose may be displaying
  feelings of insecurity. Some people have expansive hand
  gestures as part of their personality.

Mediterranean people (especially the Italians) use gestures more
than the Teutonic races and the Welsh use gestures more than the
English. Men use them more than women. They can be very powerful

in emotional speeches (have you ever seen film recordings of Adolf Hitler?) but look silly if they are forced. You should never build gestures into your speech deliberately—let them come naturally.

What to do with hands is one of the most difficult things to advise on. People never know whether to keep them still or to gesture. The best advice is to concentrate on developing an inner self-confidence and be aware of your own gestures. *Never* build them deliberately into a script like stage directions (Cue: *wave arms around here*) because it will look totally forced. If gestures are not part of your personality then don't try and make them. (See Chapter One for the comments of Harold Macmillan on the use of gestures.)

However, fidgeting can be very off-putting, and if you have an irritating habit do try and control it. These are some common bad habits found in speakers:

juggling and throwing objects
picking nails and cuticles
fiddling with rings and watches
coiling bits of hair or running hand through hair
shuffling cue cards
rustling paper
playing with coins in the pocket
scratching
clutching backs of chairs or lecterns
waving hands around in the air (this *can* be effective)
wringing hands

So what should you do with your hands? Here are eight tips.

1 Hold them lightly (not tightly) in front of you, but don't look like Norman the Nudist, as if you are trying to protect your (male) private parts.

2 Putting your hands in your pockets can look sloppy but you might want to look relaxed in which case this may be OK. Ask others for feed back if you are unsure.

3 Holding them behind your back (a habit of many men) will make you look like Prince Philip or a retired Colonel. Try and keep your hands loosely by your sides if possible.

4 Holding an object such as a pencil or felt tip market may help you to stop playing with your hands so long as you don't start fidgeting with the pencil or pen.

5 If there is a lectern you could try putting your hands firmly on it.

6. Arm gestures emanating from the elbow, and hand gestures emanating from the wrist, can look wimpish. Arm gestures should come from the shoulder and be definite, not half-hearted.

7 Avoid folding your arms in front of you: this creates a barrier.

8 If you have papers or cue cards then you can hold these—but don't fiddle them with.

Bodily movement and gesture

An upright stance with your feet planted firmly on the ground and a confident walk looks good. It's surprising how the tiniest movement can be exaggerated. If your feet turn in slightly it may make you look unsure of yourself and a slight slouch will make you look sloppy.

The first impression the audience have of you is gained the moment you walk into the room and stand in front of them. If you look pompous and too self-assured this may put them off. If you walk in with your head down looking unsure of yourself, a weak message will be communicated. Your posture and walk result from how you feel at the time.

Posture also has a particular function. An upright posture helps clear the body's airways, aids breathing, and helps you to project your voice. The Alexander Technique, developed by actor F. Matthias Alexander (1869-1955) and taught today all over the world, is based on finding correct posture.

Exercise: posture

Here is an exercise for you to try. Stand in front of a mirror with your feet about 9 inches apart and very slightly turned out. Your hands should hang loosely at your sides. Now try regular, deep breathing and see how comfortable it feels. Try and feel comfortable with your body staying still in this position.

To stand or sit?

Standing is to be recommended in most situations as it helps convey authority. However, if you wish to appear to be 'on the same level as your audience' then sitting might be more appropriate. Some teachers prefer to sit on tables swinging their legs. This, again, may help if you want to encourage the audience to participate but watch out for excessive swinging legs—they can be distracting.

If in doubt, always stand for the following reasons:

- it gives you more authority;
- it helps your breathing;
- the audience can see you better—and you can see them;
- it leaves you free to move and use gestures;
- it is easier to use audio-visual aids—you don't have to get up.

Now try putting it all together. Get a friend to watch you walk into a room, slowly and confidently, stand erect in front of your (imaginary) audience and look at them slowly before smiling and saying, 'Good afternoon.'

Audience body language
The body language of your audience can give you feedback on how your performance is being received.

Good signs:
- Agreeable nodding.
- Fixed gaze with the head on one side (they are listening).
- Sitting slightly forwards.

Bad signs:
- Fidgeting
- Looking at watches or clocks on the wall.
- Looking around the room or behind.
- Sitting back in the chair with arms behind the head. (This *may* mean that your ideas are being taken with some suspicion or disbelief.)
- Arms and legs crossed may indicate reluctance to accept your ideas (but not always).
- Frowning indicates some unhappiness with what you are saying.

Orientation
Put in plain English, orientation is all about where you place yourself in relation to others. Should you stand at the front, mingle with the audience or sit in their midst?

For a formal lecture you obviously need to be at the front, possibly on a platform. There may be technical reasons why you can't do a spontaneous 'walkabout' amongst the audience—you may have a microphone on stage which isn't mobile. In small groups think about whether you want to be perceived as 'in control' or 'one of them'. Standing or sitting behind a table will put a barrier between you and your audience—this may be appropriate in some situations and not in others. In a schoolroom, you may need to establish your authority before you start to relax and perch on the filing cabinet with your legs swinging. If you want your audience to relax and open up then you will need to be physically closer to them.

One further point. Inexperienced speakers often make the mistake of hiding behind overhead projectors and other equipment. You look up and see their face masked by the projection head. It is important to place equipment to one side and yourself centrally. (More on how to use audio-visual equipment in Chapter 8.)

CLOTHES AND GENERAL APPEARANCE

What kind of clothes should you wear? Essentially, you should wear clothes appropriate for your audience. This sounds like stating the obvious, but let's illustrate. If you are talking to an audience of sporting people or sports centre managers then wear a blazer rather than a dark suit (for males) and don't dress up *too* smartly (females). For an audience of social or voluntary workers, Jaeger or Armani suits won't go down very well because it will immediately separate you socially from your audience. If you are speaking to a room full of lawyers, accountants or company directors then you should play safe and wear your best cut suit (or dress), not slacks and a pullover. If your audience are designers then very traditional clothing may set you apart from them (which you may not want).

Clothing tips for males and females

- Avoid wearing anything brand new.

- Wear clothes you feel comfortable in whilst looking smart.

- Don't wear anything unusual which will distract the audience. This is not the occasion to wear your flashing bow tie or Carmen Miranda hat.

- Colours are important. If your background is going to be bright orange then a pink suit will look terrible. Again, if the background is light then you should wear a dark suit—and vice versa. Colours which fail to carry authority are pale pink and pale blue (baby colours). For some unknown reason, people are often advised to avoid mustard. If you have a pale skin colouring avoid beige—it will make you look very pasty. Brown and avocado green (like green wellies) are associated with the country—fine if you are talking to the National Farmers Union, not so good if you are taking to a City audience as they may not accord you any respect.

Clothing tips for women

- Keep a spare pair of tights handy. Avoid garish tights or stockings.

- Avoid a tight skirt which shows your knickers, particularly if you have to walk up steps onto a platform.

- Carry a small handbag and put it out of the way when you speak. If you can leave it somewhere before you start, so much the better.

- Jewellery should be subtle. Don't wear jangling bracelets.

- Necklines should be modest—don't show cleavage.

- Pay attention to hem lines. Are they straight? If you are on a platform then the eye line of the audience will be around your knees and they will notice bits of cotton hanging down.

- Wear medium-heeled shoes and avoid high heels.

Clothing tips for men

- Make sure your socks match. Avoid white socks or luminous colours—unless you want to make a particular statement such as 'I am a rebel'.

- Don't fill up your pockets with coins or weigh them down.

- Wear a tie for most occasions. There are, however, some situations in which you may want to look casual—a talk to independent travellers and explorers (breeches and crampons?), an informal tutorial with students or a training session for aspiring DJs.

EXERCISES

Practise reading a passage from a book (childrens' story books are good) which has a lot of illustrative passages. Read it first without gestures. Then put the book down or put it on a lectern and use your hands.

Here are some exercises. Read them aloud and see if gestures come naturally. If not, don't force them.

'This company is set for huge expansion over the next two years. We predict that output will rise and our direct competition will fall.'

'The container is shaped like a long cylinder with one end smaller than the other tapering almost to a point.'

'We are going to look at the problem from the bottom up.'

Now try reading aloud this passage from *Lord of the Rings* (Chapter 1) using some of the hints in Chapter 6 and this chapter. Make the passage come alive. Use your voice like a musical instrument and integrate gestures as an extension of your vocal range.

'There were rockets like a flight of scintillating birds singing with sweet voices. There were green trees with trunks of dark smoke: their leaves opened like a whole spring unfolding in a moment, and their shining branches dropped glowing flowers down upon the astonished hobbits, disappearing with a sweet scent just before they touched their upturned faces. There were fountains of butterflies that flew glittering into the trees, there were pillars of coloured fires that rose and turned into eagles, or sailing ships, or a phalanx of flying swans; there was a red thunderstorm and a shower of yellow rains; there was a forest of silver spears that sprang suddenly into the air with a yell like an embattled army, and came down again into the Water with a hiss like a hundred hot snakes. And there was one last surprise, in honour of Bilbo, and it startled the hobbits exceedingly, as Gandalf intended. The lights went out. A great smoke went up. It shaped itself like a mountain seen in the distance, and began to glow at the summit. It sprouted green and scarlet flames. Out flew a red-gold dragon—not life-size, but terribly life-like: fire came from his jaws, his eyes glared down; there was a roar, and he whizzed three times over the heads of the crowd. They all ducked, and many fell flat on their faces. The dragon passed like an express train, turned a somersault, and burst over Bywater with a deafening explosion.'

CHECKLIST

- The first impression is made when you walk into the room. Think positive, look straight ahead and stride in confidently.

- Before you open your mouth, pause and look at the audience— all of them. And smile.

- Make sure you look at *every* member of the audience at some stage.

- Find your way of keeping your hands still—if this is a problem try holding a pen.

- Gestures should never be forced and should never follow the key word. Synchronising gestures is vitally important.

- Get a friend to watch you when you speak or ask someone ot videotape you. Your mannerisms will come across as an audience will see them.

- If on a platform, keep still and avoid pacing up and down. However, if you are working with a smaller group then mingling with the members helps them to get involved.

- Choose your clothes carefully, especially shoes.

- And lastly (which will be dealt with in the next chapter), don't hide behind physical barriers.

'We're just not impressed by your body language!'

8
Audiovisual Aids and the Physical Environment

The other visual aspects of making a speech which you need to consider, other than your own body language and physical appearance, are the use of visual (and audio) aids, and the physical environment.

THE PHYSICAL ENVIRONMENT

Before arriving at the place where you are to speak to an audience, deliver a talk or presentation, teach a class, run a training session or speak at a meeting, you should investigate the kind of room and environment in which you will be speaking. This is something over which you have very little control. Whereas you can produce your own audio-visual aids, the room will be provided for you in most cases. However, you can request certain seating plans and you may have control over things like lighting.

Imagine the worst possible environment. (If any of you have taught or been taught in under-funded schools or institutions you may find this familiar!) The room is sparse and poorly heated. Some of the windows are cracked. A wind that reminds you of Wuthering Heights rattles the building. A slow drip is coming through the ceiling, landing with monotonous regularity in a bucket. You can hear the roar of the traffic outside. And it's cold. There may be very little you can do about this—but you could for example rearrange the furniture and make the seating a little more inviting.

Seating
There are basically six common seating arrangements. You may be asked if you want:

1 theatre style   seats in rows as in a theatre
2 classroom style   seats in rows with tables or desks

3 boardroom/meeting style	one table with seats around it
4 U-shape	3-sided table arrangement
5 semi-circle	as above without tables
6 workshop groups	small tables with 4-8 at each table scattered around the room

The layout you need will depend upon the size of audience, the nature of the session (formal/informal) and the shape of the room.

SEATING PLANS

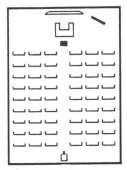

1/ THEATRE STYLE
SUITABLE FOR CONFERENCES OR LECTURES WITH LITTLE PARTICIPATION. (FIXED BENCHES FOR NOTE TAKING OPTIONAL)

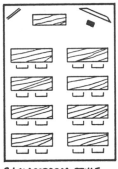

2/ CLASSROOM STYLE
LIMITED PARTICIPATION BUT MAKES NOTE TAKING EASIER THAN THEATRE STYLE

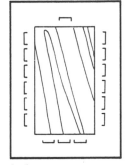

3/ BOARDROOM OR MEETING STYLE

4/ SEMINAR STYLE
MORE DISCUSSION THAN IN CLASSROOM STYLE BUT GROUPS NEED TO BE SMALLER

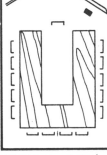

5/ INFORMAL STYLE/ DISCUSSION GROUP
IDEAL FOR DISCUSSION WITH LITTLE NOTE TAKING

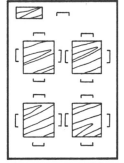

6/ WORKSHOP STYLE/ INFORMAL CLASSROOM
BEST SUITED TO PEOPLE WORKING IN SMALL GROUPS WHERE ROLE OF LEADER IS MINIMAL

CHAIRS

LECTERN

OHP

SCREEN

PROJECTOR

FLIP CHART

TABLE

A word about chairs—try and find comfortable ones with soft seats. It is really difficult to sit on hard seats for too long. If you are doing physical activities make sure you can move the chairs and tables around without too much difficulty.

The way you arrange the seating will affect the kind of session you want to run. Do you want people to interact?—then don't seat them classroom or theatre style. Do you want them to take notes?—then give them tables. If you want to remain fully in control then theatre or classroom style is probably best.

Always make sure that everyone can see you. One problem with the semi-circle is that the people at the edge can feel left out. Make sure you look at them frequently (see the previous chapter on **eye contact**). If you are using visual aids you will also need to check that everyone can see those.

Lighting

If you can control this, so much the better. Ideal surroundings will have spotlights, dimmers and a pleasant environment. Fluorescent lighting can actually interfere with the connections between the two hemispheres of the brain and reduce concentration—and if they flicker this is *very* irritating.

Always check lighting if you are using slides, film or an overhead projector. Some classrooms or community centre halls do not have blackout, which is particularly important when using slides (but not with overhead projectors).

Heating and ventilation

Your audience is sure to complain if the room is too hot or too cold more readily if you bore them to death. Be aware of temperature. If people are uncomfortable they won't listen to you. Air conditioning units can rattle and hum and distract the audience; make sure you know how to turn them off. Ask your audience whether they are comfortable and if the temperature is OK—their welfare is important. Open a few windows after a while if the room is getting stuffy.

Acoustics and noise

Outside noise—traffic, children, heavy footsteps—distract the audience, particularly if they are doing work that calls for concentration. It doesn't help if, at the critical moment in your speech when you pause for dramatic effect, a loud voice outside the door yells, 'Come on Darren, get a bloody move on!' Check out the room at different times of the day. If there is a school opposite, be prepared for thunderous noise and screaming around 3.45pm. Finally, some hotels have the annoying habit of running fire drills in the middle of seminars. Check first.

Acoustics may be critical in a large room or hall, particularly if you are using music or recorded sound. Remember that people absorb sound—your voice will not carry so far when the room is full.

Microphones

If you have never used a microphone before, do practise first. Microphones have the annoying habit of breaking down. They can hum and shriek and do all kinds of funny things. You will need someone standing by just in case. *Don't* start by saying 'one two three. Can you hear me at the back?' That should all be done beforehand when the room is empty. However, you could have a friend at the back signalling if the microphone doesn't work. Don't shout into the microphone. Be prepared to make do without one if needed.

Power points

Find out where these are beforehand. There is nothing more annoying than setting up a slide projector only to find that the flex doesn't reach. Conference centres shouldn't present any problems, but classrooms and church halls are apt to have a single socket at the opposite end of the room to where you need it. Carry an extension lead with you just in case, or ask to borrow one.

A final point about rooms in general. If you are in a position to request certain rooms then be quite clear as to what you need. Seminars and workshops often need two rooms—one for the general sessions and an adjoining room for small group work. L-shaped rooms are difficult for large groups. Make sure you have a separate room for lunch and coffee—or keep this area well away from the main activities.

And lastly, don't forget **orientation**—think about where you want to stand or sit in relation to your audience (see Chapter 7).

We are now going to look at audio and visual aids. It is *very* important to allow plenty of time to set up a room if you are using moveable aids. Arrive *at least* one hour beforehand.

AUDIO VISUAL AIDS

Audio and visual aids can greatly enhance a presentation. However, they cannot make up for a poor speaker; if used badly even the best equipment can make the speaker look quite unprofessional.

First of all, you don't *have* to use audio and visual aids. There are plenty of brilliant speakers who rarely use them. Politicians seem to manage without, so do preachers. If used badly they can get in the way. However, remember that people absorb information through *all* their senses; using visual or audio aids can increase your impact considerably and help people remember what you have said. Be clear on why you are using them. Is it to:

—reinforce what you are saying?
—illustrate points that would be difficult with words alone?
—help the audience to remember the main points?
—or simply to make the speech more entertaining and lively?

Here are some examples of situations in which visuals are useful or necessary:

- To show diagrammatically how a machine works.
- To show the layout of a store, house or floor plans of a building.
- In a sales presentation, to focus the attention of the audience.
- For an illustrated lecture on fine art.
- For a technical or mathematical subject where figures are involved.
- Where you want the audience to participate by producing information which you then write down.
- If the concepts are difficult to take in by listening—legal lectures for example often need visual back-up or handouts.
- If you are at a meeting to discuss proposals which the delegates need to see in order to absorb the information.

The main kinds of visual and audio aids are:

blackboards
whiteboards
flipcharts
overhead projectors
handouts
slides
film
video
posters, charts
physical objects
recorded sound (disc or tape)

Add to this list the latest technology in computerised presentation kits which provide high-resolution graphics on screen with moving graphs and images that glide smoothly from one visual to the next.

Blackboards (or 'chalkboards')

Advantages
- Easy to use and wipe.
- Good for building up ideas as you go along—keeps the audience's attention.

Disadvantages
- Reminds people of school.
- Looks unprofessional
- Messy – dust gets everywhere.
- Can't use if sensitive equipment is around. (Too much dust).
- Difficult to read
- Can't store information when the board gets full.
- You need to turn your back to the audience.

Hints and points to watch
- Squeaky chalk and fingernail scraping – ouch.
- Shiny board – difficult to read.
- You may lose chalk or find there isn't a duster available.
- You may find it difficult to write on a vertical surface.
- Avoid blackboards if at all possible.

Whiteboards

Advantages
- Similar to blackboards, without being quite as messy and without the schoolroom associations.

Disadvantages
- Can't store the information once it gets full (as with blackboards).
- If the pens dry up you are stuck.
- Some people write on whiteboards with permanent marker pens which are extremely difficult to wipe off without special chemicals.
- The writing may be too thin and difficult to read.
- The boards need wiping carefully.

Hints and points to watch
- It is useful to have a whiteboard in the room when you need to build up an argument step by step or show the workings of

formulae. Anticipation is good for keeping the audience on their toes. However, you must have good pens and make sure the board is clean before you start. *And don't use permanent markers.*

Flipcharts

Advantages
- You can prepare everything beforehand at home and bring it with you.
- They are flexible—you can also use them to write on whilst speaking, you can flick from page to page, tear pages off and so on.
- Information can be stored.
- They don't get messy or need cleaning.
- They can be moved around the room.
- Delegates/students can use flipcharts to record their own comments during group sessions.
- Pages can be torn off and distributed for discussion.

Disadvantages
- Difficult to read at the back of a large room (as are chalkboards and whiteboards).
- Not a lot of space in which to write.
- Can be awkward to use—pages get stuck and rustle.
- Easy to knock over.

Hints and points to watch
- If you are not used to flipcharts prepare them carefully beforehand. Sketch out each page in pencil before writing with a marker pen in case you run out of space. Is your writing large and bold enough? Use fat marker pens.
- Consider the order—do you want to start at the back and work through to the front? (It can be easier to pull pages forward than push them back.)
- Dog-ear the corner of each sheet to make it easier to turn over. It can look very unprofessional if you are just about to come to your punch line, which is written on the next page, and you fumble around trying to push the page back.
- Can everyone see the flipchart? Try it in different positions.
- Which different colours could you use for impact?
- Don't get over-excited—you may knock the stand over.
- If you are writing on the flipchart as you go along, you may find yourself in a bent knee position as you reach the bottom of the page. This looks very undignified—and you need strong legs.

- Stand to one side when writing. Which side suits you best?
- Don't talk while you are writing (this also applies when using chalkboards and whiteboards).
- Use key words only rather than full text.
- Don't make the page too busy.
- Having a blank sheet just before an important point creates anticipation. How about leaving one sheet blank between sections so that when you are talking about a different subject you don't have words on the flipchart that refer to something else?
- Want a real dramatic impact?—try ripping one page off the stand as you make your point.
- Flipcharts are useful for group sessions. Could you distribute pages to each group to write their key points on and then hang them around the walls with Blu-tack?

Overhead projectors

Advantages
- The OHP gives a clear image which can be seen in a large room.
- Materials can be prepared beforehand.
- The size of image can be enlarged or reduced simply by moving the projector.
- It looks professional as the text/images can be printed and prepared professionally.
- Flexibility—the OHP can be used to write on during a session.
- Transparencies can be arranged in any order and changed easily. (Not so easy with slides.)
- Relatively cheap and easy to prepare.
- You can overlay transparencies and build up a picture.
- The presenter doesn't have to turn his back on the audience.
- Blackout is not required—can be used in any room.
- OHPs are not as messy as chalkboards.

Disadvantage
- Large and bulky to carry around.
- The image can get distorted.
- Presenters are tempted to hide behind them.

Hints and points to watch
- Are you sure you know how to use it? Try it out first. The mirror on the projection head needs to be tilted before you will get any light on the screen and you will need to adjust the focus.

- The image can get distorted if the OHP is placed too much at an angle.
- Don't lean on the projection head or you may find yourself moving slowly toward the floor as it slides down.
- Tilt the screen slightly down towards the floor.
- Position the projector on a low table if possible and put the screen on a corner rather than in the middle.
- Check to see if people at the back can read the screen. If not, move the projector so that the text is larger.
- Have your transparency in place *before* you switch on the projector. Don't switch on to a blank screen and then put your transparency down. You can keep it switched on once you have started but try and slide the next transparency on as soon as you have taken the previous one off.
- Arrange your transparencies in the right order beforehand.
- If you want to pause and talk, and you don't need people to focus on the screen, SWITCH OFF.
- Keep a 'hard' paper copy in front of you so you don't have to turn around whilst talking about what's on the screen.
- Point things out on the transparency rather than the screen.
- Give people time to read and absorb what's on the screen. Don't whip off one transparency and slap the next one on too quickly.
- Use a piece of paper to cover points if you want to reveal them one at a time. But remember to cover everything before you switch on. (This practice irritates some people, unfortunately.)
- Carry a spare bulb with you or make sure there is one available.

After a while, you will begin to feel at home with this kind of equipment and will develop slickness, but it can be overused and it looks terrible if you don't know how to use it.

Preparing overhead transparencies

1 Waterproof, permanent pens should be used when preparing transparencies.

2 Water-soluble pens should be used when you want to wipe the transparency afterwards.

3 Print size needs to be larger than a typewriter. If you have access to a desk-top publishing or graphics system this is ideal.

4 When writing on transparencies, make sure your writing is legible and looks professional.

5 Don't cram too much onto the transparency. Use key words and talk around them. You can use a handout with more information on as a back-up.

6 Frame up your transparency with a cardboard frame. This ensures that the platen (flat part on which you place the transparency) is covered and it makes it easier for you to separate the transparencies.

7 Special transparencies for use in photocopiers can be bought. This enables you to copy from the printed page straight onto the transparency. However, you *must* check you have the right kind of materials or you will gunge up the photocopier. Ordinary transparencies will melt. An alternative system is to use a heat transfer machine.

8 Arrange your transparencies in the right order beforehand.

9 Keep a 'hard' paper copy in front of you so you don't have to turn around whilst talking about what's on the screen.

10 Use coloured transparencies and coloured pens.

Slides

Advantages
- Slides look very professional.
- Almost anything can be reproduced; you can use high quality photography and illustrations.
- Slides show detail well.
- Slides use colour to good effect.
- Ideal in a large auditorium.
- Dramatic impact.

Disadvantages
- Can be expensive to prepare.
- Need a darkened room with good blackout (in most cases).
- You lose contact with the audience because they can't see you.
- Carousel projectors sometimes 'swallow' slides or get stuck.
- You can't change the order of slides easily.

Hints and points to watch when using slides
- Mark each slide with a dot to indicate which way round it should go into the carousel or slide carriage. Rehearse first.
- Allow plenty of time to set up your equipment.

- Make sure the size of image on screen is appropriate for the size of audience.
- Place the screen in the centre of the room and the projector in the centre aisle (unless you are using back projection).
- Two projectors will make your presentation flow better and avoid having blank screens, but you will need a good technical assistant. For a really professional presentation, a dissolve unit (if you can get hold of one) is superb.
- Make sure you can use the remote control button and you know which way is forward and which way is back.
- Get your slides in the right order and have them clearly marked on your script so you know where you are.

Preparing slides
Slides can be prepared by professional slide makers, or you can make your own by placing your original on a flat surface, lighting it and photographing it onto 35mm transparencies.

Bear the following in mind. (Many of these points also apply to making OHP transparencies.)

- Use typesizes larger than ordinary typewriter size.
- Stick to legible typefaces such as Helvetica or Times Roman. Avoid elaborate lettering.
- Use bullet points and key words rather than lengthy script which is difficult to absorb.
- Be consistent in your use of underlinings, bold type or headings.
- Statistics are hard to take in. Use graphs, pie charts and other visuals. See artwork.
- Use colours to separate up different points. Coloured backgrounds have impact, but don't overdo it. Use four colours maximum.
- White writing on black has more impact than black on white.
- Don't use more than six lines on one slide.
- Blank slides (black) between sections help to break things up and are useful when you need to make a quick break to explain something.

Note: There are some very sophisticated systems which involve back projection onto screens and a computer-based system which enables images to be projected onto a screen from a computer graphics system.

Some useful contacts

Advertising, Music, Film & Videotape Producers Association,
26 Noel Street, London W1V 3RD.

Association of Professional Video Makers, 24 Highbury
Grove, London N5 2EA. Tel: (0171) 354 0776.

Audio Visual Association, 46 Manor View, London N3 2SR.
Tel: (0181) 349 2429.

British Association of Picture Libraries, 13 Woodberry
Crescent, London N10 1PJ. Tel: (081) 444 7913.

British Film Institute, 21 Stephen St, London W1P 1PL. Tel:
(0171) 255 1444. The BFI is a member of the International
Federation of Film Archives.

Educational Television Association, The King's Manor,
Exhibition Square, York YO1 2EP. Tel: (01904) 29701.

International Visual Communications Association (IVCA),
Bolsover House, 5/6 Clipstone Street, London W1P 7EB.

National Association for Higher Education in Film and Video,
64 Nortoft Road, Chalfont St Peter, Bucks SL9 OLD.

Performing Right Society, 29 Berners Street, London W1P
4AA. Tel: (0171) 580 5544.

Film and video

Pre-recorded material on film or video is extremely useful to illustrate
or liven up a lecture or presentation. It has the advantage of being
able to show things that would be difficult just by using words.
However, film and video can be overused.

Advantages
- Grabs audience attention quickly.
- Can illustrate in a way that still images can't. Good for showing
  how things work and hearing comments from people.
- Incorporates sound and commentary.
- Shows things 'as they happen'.
- Good for introducing humour and vitality.
- You can take advantage of professional presentation experts and
  'personalities'.
- Useful for breaking up sessions.
- The presenter can have a temporary rest.

Disadvantages
- Needs to be exactly relevant or it can be seen as a 'toy'.
- Expensive to hire and buy films and videos.

- Loss of personal contact with the audience.
- Films are prone to breaking down and are noisy. (Video is better and easier to use.)
- TV sets can go wrong.

Hints and points to watch
- *Always* check the film or video beforehand. The TV set may not be tuned in properly, the sound might not be switched on and other things may not work. Check.
- Locate the beginning of the tape (or the point at which you want to start) beforehand.
- Don't overdo it or your audience will think you are copping out. Half an hour of video (or film) is probably enough.
- Make sure the video is relevant to your main point and not just entertainment.
- The content should be pitched appropriately for your audience. Don't show a schools programme to an adult group.

A word about using video cameras to record people in interview situations, meetings, or doing presentations: this is a highly effective aid in training sessions as it can illustrate all kinds of idiosyncracies and help people to present themselves better. However, anyone trying to use it should make sure they know how the equipment works. It looks so unprofessional when a trainer or teacher fumbles with cameras and video equipment. The secret is to practise beforehand and make sure that the camera is switched to RECORD for recording and PLAYBACK for playback. (The camera may have other words such as CAMERA and VIDEO—make sure you know what they mean.)

Handouts
Using handout material (usually typed sheets) is valuable when you don't have the time to go into depth, you want the audience to have some permanent record of what you have said, or written notes are needed for revision.

Advantages
- You can write down detail and complicated information which would be too much for a lecture session or talk.
- People can take away a permanent record of what you have said.
- It looks professional: the audience feel they have got value-for-money.
- It reinforces learning and helps revision.

Disadvantages
- Handouts can distract the audience from what you are saying. If you want them to listen first you will need to leave the handout material until later.
- It can stop them paying attention if they think they are going to get it all later. (This applies mainly to students.)
- If handed out during a session this can be disruptive and it takes a long time. People have the irritating habit of taking one page and not another. It can take ten minutes to sort everyone out with the right pages.

Hints and points to watch
- Staple or clip everything together beforehand. It saves time and trouble getting pages sorted out.
- Either   put down key points and give them out ·during the session so that people can take their own notes as you speak,

  Or   talk generally and say you are giving handouts with the detail later,

  Or   try variations on both.
- People don't always read handout material afterwards. If you are seeing the audience again then you may have to refresh their minds or ask them to do an assignment which makes them read the material.

Physical objects
Objects such as antiques, paintings, pieces of equipment and examples of products are very useful as they represent 'the real things', not just a photograph.

Advantages
- Real, not simulated.
- People can handle them and walk around them.
- Adds interest.
- Can be picked up. This gives impact to a presentation if the actual object is there, in the speaker's hand.

Disadvantages
- Small objects are difficult for a large audience to see.
- They can be distracting.
- Can be bulky to carry around.
- Security (if the objects are valuable).

Hints and points to watch
- Put objects aside or cover them up when you are not talking about them or the audience will focus on the object and not you.
- Don't hand around an object whilst you are talking: it's guaranteed to stop the audience listening to what you are saying. Better to let them look at the object during a break.

Audio aids

This includes the use of audio tapes, records and compact discs. Generally audio aids are underused. However, they can be extremely effective when teaching drama, giving talks about history or, naturally, music talks or lectures where they are essential.

Background music is sometimes used in training sessions to help people relax and open up the 'right' side of the brain.

Advantages
- You can use professional presenters or actors to make points.
- Sound and music can be very effective to create atmosphere.
- Pre-recorded commentary for use with slides works well sometimes, particularly when music is used.

Disadvantages
- You'll need good quality equipment.
- Difficult to locate the exact spot you need on some discs/tapes.
- Pre-recorded commentary with visuals means you lose contact with the audience and cannot make your own comments.
- Recording takes a long time.
- Some people cannot concentrate on recordings for long.

Hints and points to watch
- Check the quality of the equipment and volume beforehand.
- If you are using a number of discs or sound recorded on tape, make sure you have everything in the right order and that you can locate the right spot easily. Recording onto reel-to-reel tape with coloured leader tape in between each part may help.
- When recording material yourself use high quality equipment and a good microphone.

WHAT CAN GO WRONG?

Just about *anything* can go wrong! It is important to be well prepared and not rattled by acts of God or complete disasters.

What if there is a power cut or electrical failure?
Yes, this can sometimes happen. If your entire presentation is built around visual aids you are in trouble! Possible solutions:

- Change the order; talk or introduce group activities until the power is restored (assuming it's temporary).
- See it as a challenge and share the joke with the audience (who will be sympathetic, as the fault is not with you).
- Transfer to the flipchart if you can.
- Abandon the event until power is restored. (Not possible if people have come a long way or they have paid to hear you).
- Move to another room or building.

What if the OHP or slide projector packs up?
The most common problems are a bulb failing or a loose connection at the plug.

- Find a technician quickly and move onto the next topic.
- Take an early tea/coffee break.
- Try and fix it yourself, or enlist a member of the audience. (Take a spare bulb and screwdriver with you.)

Bulbs blow frequently. Carousel projectors often get stuck or slides fly out, usually because the carousel isn't positioned properly. Carry a spare carousel for emergencies.

What if the video doesn't work?
This is likely to result from incorrect tuning. To use video you need to know which **channel** to use and make sure the TV monitor is tuned to **video**. Check out thoroughly beforehand. It is particularly important to go through everything if you are using closed-circuit TV with playback facilities. Video cameras have a switch for **playback** and another for **record**. If you are not switched to the right one the camera won't record or play back—and you will look a real fool in front of your audience.

Most other disasters can be avoided through careful preparation. However, when they *do* happen, do avoid getting flustered. Calmness and a sense of humour are essential if you are to sail through the disaster without losing the audience. Try some phrases like:
'Never trust equipment that's hired.'
'Maybe if you all shout at once the power will come on.'
'Do we have a technician in the audience?'

Checklist when preparing visuals
- Try out all visuals on the equipment and check for size, legibility and ease of reading at the back of the room.
- Don't use too many words on your visuals.
- Avoid statistics in table form. Use graphics, bar charts, pie charts and other illustrations.
- Make sure your visuals are numbered and in the right order.
- Do you have the right pens and markers? Have a range of both permanent and water-soluble markers in different colours and thicknesses.
- Do your OHP transparencies smudge easily? Then you need to use permanent marker pens. Get your OHP transparencies produced on a desk-top publishing or computer graphics system if possible.
- Can you absorb one visual easily? If using statistics, will the audience be able to take them in?
- Are your audio-visual aids really relevant, or are you using them as gimmicks?
- Are you making use of blank pages or blank slides between sections whilst you need to talk?

Checklist when setting up the room and equipment
- Arrive at least one hour beforehand and be prepared to move furniture and equipment.
- Check location of plug sockets.
- Do you have an extension lead handy?
- Set up the screen so that it tilts slightly downwards.
- Make sure you are 'centre stage' and that the visual aids don't dominate too much.
- Can you move easily between OHP, flipchart and slide projector if you need to, without tripping over flex and equipment?
- Can everyone read your visuals? Have you tried every spot in the room?
- Have you tested the dimmer switches? Is there someone to operate them?
- Do you have enough pens and markers?
- Are your OHP transparencies in the right order and easy to get hold of? Keep them next to the OHP on a table.
- Are your handouts in the right order so you don't have to hunt for them before giving them out?
- Does the TV or video camera work?
- Is the video cassette at the right place for starting? (You don't

want trailers or the tail end of the last programme.)
- If using audio, is the equipment set up properly? Have you tested it? Is the tape at the right spot?
- If using a microphone, try it out.
- Final check to see if everything works.

EXERCISE

Suggest the most appropriate audio or visual aid plus room seating for use in presentation about each of the following.

Subject   *Audience*

1 Showing the new layout of an office.   Small group of
                                            employees (about 12).

2 Presenting a cost breakdown   As above.
   for your department.

3 Explaining how to deal with a   Young trainees in a
   difficult customer.   company (about 20).

4 Presenting a proposed advertising   Small client group
   campaign to a potential client.   (about 6 people).

5 Teaching the best way to use a   Group of students (20).
   piece of electronic equipment.

6 Giving a talk on antiques.   Women's Institute (40).

7 Presenting the case for buying   Board of Directors.
   a computer system.

8 Talking about marketing into   Audience of 100+.
   Eastern Europe at a conference.

9 Launching a new product (kitchen   The press (could be any
   gadget) at a press conference.   size).

For suggested answers see page 155.

9
Preparing Yourself and Dealing with Nerves

The big day is looming. You have written up your presentation, planned for the lecture or seminar, prepared the visuals and have some idea of what the audience will be expecting.

You will need a run through to check timing and to see how the audio-visual aids work.

REHEARSING

Stage one
Read or talk through your speech. Time it. Remember that in reality you may speed up or slow down. Always try and slow down if possible: people tend to talk too fast when nervous. Most people talk at between 150 and 200 words a minute. (John F. Kennedy spoke at the rate of about 300 words a minute). Make allowances for audio-visual aids and give time for the audience to absorb visuals.

Stage two
Now go back to your notes and revise them, taking into account the timing. You may need to cut out something or add a bit. As you go through, make sure you can answer the following questions:

- Are my objectives clear?
- When I stop talking I want the audience to...
- Can I sum up what I am trying to put across in a single sentence?
- Have I used illustrations and anecdotes which are relevant?
- Do my opening words grab attention?
- Have I made a suitable conclusion?
- If I am intending to use jokes can I carry this off without embarrassment? Are the jokes relevant?

If you are reading a script rather than talking from cue cards, make sure that you have written it in *spoken* English. (See Chapter 5.) Mark certain words for emphasis and mark in the pauses. Some people make comments in the margin such as 'Argument weak— shout like blazes' (a Methodist minister referring to a sermon he was having difficulty with). If you are speaking from cue cards, the rehearsal will test their effectiveness as a prompt.

Stage three

Now read or talk it through again, incorporating all the audio-visual aids. Tape record yourself if you can. If you are using a flipchart you will need to practise pushing the pages back and writing on them. Make sure your script or cue cards are clearly marked. This time, try and imagine you are in a room full of people or get a friend to act as 'guinea pig'. Time it again. Your timing should be within 3 minutes of your time slot. If in doubt, it is better to run under time than talk for too long. You will probably speed up anyway when you start.

Stage four

Finally, make sure your cue cards are clearly numbered and tagged together (if you are using cue cards), the pages of your speech are clearly numbered (if you are reading your speech) and your writing or typing is legible. Sheets of paper should not be stapled together.

Working from a lesson plan

If you are planning a lecture, training session or lesson, then your preparation will be different. You are unlikely to be reading from a script or from cue cards; instead you will probably use a rough lesson plan. Experienced teachers generally don't have a written plan—they carry it in their head. In any case, teachers rarely have time to prepare as thoroughly as you will have to for a speech or presentation. If you are new to teaching or lecturing, however, you may find it necessary to go through the four stages of rehearsal.

CHECKING OUT YOUR VENUE

If you don't have time to visit the venue personally, then make sure you know the following before you start.

– The exact location and roughly how long it will take you to get there. There is nothing worse than being stuck in a traffic jam arriving in a state of tension. Always allow extra time for delays and always ask for directions, to be on the safe side.

- The name or number of the room (it saves you having to walk around the building aimlessly).
- The size and shape of the room.
- Number and location of power points.
- Where to park and how to get equipment into the building (if you need to).
- Where the light and dimmer switches are (and who will operate them).
- What equipment is available and what you need to bring.
- The kind of furniture there is in the room.
- The timing of breaks for tea, coffee and lunch.
- The availability of a Public Address (PA) system and microphone.

PACKING YOUR KIT BAG

Having some kind of bag or 'box of tricks' will save you all kinds of embarrassment if it turns out that the venue doesn't have proper equipment and stationery. This may sound a little paranoid—like taking the entire contents of your medicine box away with you for a short holiday in Spain—but in the words of the scout song, it's better to BE PREPARED.

Checklist of accessories

- Large felt marker pens in four different colours.
- Set of permanent marker pens (finer) in different colours.
- Set of water-soluble marker pens in different colours.
- Pens and pencils.
- Ruler.
- A4 paper—plain and lined.
- Acetate sheets.
- Blu-tack.
- Sellotape.
- Masking tape.
- Drawing pins.
- Paper clips.
- Screwdriver.
- Extension lead.
- Spare bulb for overhead projector and slide projector.
- Index cards.
- Stapler.
- Spare pairs of tights (for women).
- Aspirin or pain killers.
- Paper hankies.

DEALING WITH NERVES

Why is it that speaking in public is such a terrifying experience for a lot of people? It is probably because the persona is exposed—it's like standing naked in a room full of people. Every eye is on you and if you are not used to this it can be extremely intimidating. In her book *Effective Speaking* Christina Stuart cites a survey conducted in the USA, where 3,000 people were asked to list their ten worst fears. Speaking in public came out as the number one fear—worse than spiders, snakes, and even financial ruin and death.

It may reassure you to know that many experienced actors suffer from nerves and 'stage fright'. The late Laurence Olivier went through a period of being transfixed with terror before every performance. Many other actors and experienced speakers suffer equally from nerves. Most of them, however, learn how to conceal those nerves.

How do people react to stress?
Think back to the last time you felt really nervous or afraid. What actually happened to you physically? Did your heart beat faster? Maybe you came out in a sweat, got butterflies in your stomach, you felt sick, your hands went clammy, your throat dried up, you felt faint and your breathing became shallow. Try and isolate exactly what *you* feel like under stress.

Most people experience identical reactions to things like a sudden loud noise. Research carried out in the 1960s by Dr Frank Pierce Jones in the USA showed that we all tighten our neck muscles, hold our breath and contract at joints in our bodies. This reaction is called 'the startle pattern'. Since most of us experience some degree of stress in our daily life, these reactions are almost habitual. When was the last time you were in a car and someone cut you up on the road? When did you last fail to see traffic lights until you were almost upon them? Did you experience any of the symptoms mentioned? Some people go into the startle pattern every time the phone rings. The problem is that these reactions are unconscious and seemingly beyond our control. The very thought of speaking in public can cause some people to tighten their throat, breathe awkwardly and stiffen up. The result is that they *sound* nervous because the airways are constricted and their breathing has become irregular.

Greville Janner MP admits to feeling a little nervous himself before he has to make a speech in the House of Commons. He stresses the *positive* aspects of nerves. 'It's only when you are nervous that the adrenalin flows,' he says. 'The skill is not showing that you are nervous.'

In his training sessions Mr Janner teaches the importance of eye contact and correct breathing as a technique for dealing with the physical symptoms of nervousness. 'Breathing techniques need to be taught properly, or people may hyperventilate and feel faint. It is important to learn to breathe deeply through the mouth and breathe out through the nose. About ten seconds before I am due to speak I take deep breaths, then stand up and pause.'

Curing nervousness involves two things. Firstly, you need to understand exactly what makes you nervous. And secondly, you need to develop techniques for controlling the physical reactions to fear.

Understanding the causes of fear

Try and visualise yourself making a speech in public or performing on stage. What exactly is it that makes your afraid? Is it the fear of 'forgetting your lines'? Perhaps you feel intimidated by having lots of people staring at you. Or maybe it's the dislike of people judging or criticising you?

Let's say that the worst fear is that of forgetting your lines or losing your place in the script. Now ask yourself: 'Does it really *matter* if this happens?' You may have witnessed this happening to someone else. It wasn't such a terrible experience for them, was it? Did you feel supportive towards the poor hapless person lost for words? You almost certainly did. So will *your* audience feel towards you.

So what would you do if you did lose your place and dried up? Have a number of techniques up your sleeve. One is to be honest and say, 'I'm sorry, I have lost my place. Could you bear with me for a moment whilst I find it?' Another is to pause and look at the audience. They won't know you are lost for words. Another is to move onto the next point or use a visual aid. Finally, have a glass of water handy—it can lubricate your throat and give you time to think.

However, the most important thing to remember is that it really doesn't matter too much if you do dry up. Your life won't change— and it's certainly very far from the worst thing that could happen to you!

Visualising and positive thinking

One way of dealing with nerves is to use the techniques of positive thinking and visualisation.

Try and visualise yourself again. See yourself walking confidently into a large room and onto a platform. You are looking good. As you walk onto the platform you feel a warmth coming from the audience. They are looking forward to what you have to say. You are surrounded by friends. However, there are one or two people you find a little intimidating. Try and imagine them in a ridiculous situation—with an onion growing out of their head, or sitting on a potty. (This works well in smaller situations such as panel interviews.) You are a great speaker and you are really going to enjoy yourself.

Try another exercise. Remember a time when you did something really well—when you excelled. It could be winning a race at school, or your wedding day, or a time you were offered a job. Try and re-create the feelings you had then. What did you feel in your stomach? What was your breathing like? Can you reproduce these again? Visualise what happened. Now try and transfer these feelings and images (or sounds) to the new situation. This may take a bit of practice but it does work.

Breathing

Training yourself to breathe correctly is the other key to overcoming nerves. Nerves are a physical reaction to a fear in the mind. You imagine yourself in a situation and the body reacts. This reaction—irregular breathing, sickness, palpitations—makes you sound nervous. Controlling the physical symptoms is the key.

Refer back to Chapter 6 to the section on breathing and the Alexander Technique. The actor F. Matthias Alexander discovered, by watching himself in the mirror, that as soon as he began to *think* about speaking in public his neck muscles would tighten, he pulled back his head, his breathing became irregular and he appeared to become shorter. This reaction has already been mentioned as 'the startle pattern'.

Suggested exercises
Try these breathing and relaxation exercises about five minutes before you are due to speak. Some of these cannot be done in public, so use your discretion.

- Take a deep breath through the nose by expanding the dia-phragm (not the chest). Let it out slowly through the mouth.
- Yawn.
- Waggle your jaw.
- Lie down on the floor with your head supported by a couple of books and try to stretch your spine.
- Screw up your face. Relax.
- Tighten your fists. Relax.

- Sit up straight and make sure your head sits straight on your shoulders without tilting back. (If you tilt it back your voice will sound strained as the airways become blocked.)
- Shake your arms and hands. Become like a rag doll.
- Hunch your shoulders and shorten your neck. Relax.
- Roll your shoulders back and then forward.
- Move your head from side to side and then round in a circle.
- Go through the vowel sounds A E I O U making your mouth as mobile as possible. Try humming up and down the musical scale.
- Go out for a brisk walk or jog to get your circulation going.
- Have a drink of water.

FINAL CHECKS ON THE DAY

When you arrive at the venue, hopefully well in advance, you should make some final checks and get the feel for the audience.

Checking the room and equipment

— Is the furniture in the right place? (See Chapter 7 and 9).
— Are the audio-visual aids in the right place for the audience and for your convenience? (See Chapter 8).
— Have you located the power points?
— Is there a good sized table for you to put your handouts and other materials on?
— Is the temperature right?
— What about ventilation?
— If you are using a microphone, does it work?
— Have you tested it?
— Does all your equipment work?
— Overhead projectors?
— Carousel/slide projector?
— Tape recorder or record player?
— Have you focused the overhead projector?
— Do you need an extension lead?
— Is there someone who can operate lights and dimmer switches for you?
— Is your flipchart prepared? Can people see it at the back?
— Have you tried out slides to check they are the right way round?
— Have you got enough pens?
— Is there a glass and jug of water handy?

Other checks

— Are your papers and transparencies in order?
— Have you found out who is in the audience and what organisations they are from? It is always useful to mingle with the audience; you can get a feel for what they are expecting and this helps you to relieve last minute nerves.
— Have you read the papers that day? Announcements in the news are both useful to include in your speech and they may affect what you intend to say.
— Do you know who you will be sharing the platform with?

Preparing yourself

Try and avoid speaking on an empty stomach—something light to eat is advisable. However, don't drink alcohol unless you *really* can't face an audience without a quick swig.

You've a few minutes to go. Make a last minute visit to the toilet, comb your hair, check your make-up and look for ladders in tights (for women). Smile. Take a few deep breaths. And make your entrance confidently.

Even if you are trembling with nerves they will go away. Relax and enjoy it. Your audience certainly will.

'Didn't you used to teach me communication skills?'

10
Putting It All Together

Now's the time to put into practice everything you have learned. In spite of meticulous planning (and the importance of this cannot be underestimated), doing it for real rarely turns out the way you planned. There is that unpredictable factor called 'the audience'. People sometimes get an attack of nerves (which invariably disappear as soon as they start talking); the audience feedback you were relying on falls flat (they turn out to be excruciatingly dull and passive individuals); or you get one person who constantly interrupts and heckles from the back. Then your equipment breaks down.

How you perform on the day will have much to do with your preparation, but audiences tend to have a 'personality' (as all stage actors will tell you) and you will need to be sensitive to their moods.

You also have a personality. Sadly, speakers often seem to lose their personality once they are in front of an audience and just perform like robots. One of the problems is too much reliance on a script which has been written like an essay. It is very important to try and be yourself and not to 'act' a part.

Take a leaf from the book of the radio presenters. One of the techniques some of them use is to imagine they are talking to one person or a small group, literally, by visualising those people in front of them. Try reading a radio script or children's story as if you were talking to just one person and then see how your delivery becomes much more natural.

MAKING AN ENTRANCE

Your entrance should be confident and deliberate. As you walk in, look around and see how they are dressed—smart dark suits, jeans and bomber jackets, flat sandals and cardigans? The clues should give you an indication as to their sensitivities, political leanings and so on.

You can get a 'feel' for an audience very quickly. In any case, you should have found out a few details of your audience beforehand.

When you turn to face your audience stand firmly on your feet, take a deep breath and pause while you make eye contact. Smile. And begin.

DELIVERY

All the lessons you have learned about how to make your voice easy to listen to and the importance of body language now come together. The problem is making enough eye contact whilst reading a script or looking at cue cards. Make sure you look up at the end of each point or paragraph to maintain eye contact—and make full use of the pause.

Timing and the pause

'The greatest magic is the pause,' says Greville Janner MP. He recommends the use of a pause after the opening statement, in mid-sentence, after an interruption or before the final words. Here are some examples:

'Ladies and gentlemen (*pause*). I am very happy to be here today.' (*pause*).

'And after all that effort and sweat, we have achieved... (*pause*) ...nothing.'

'We have here tonight (*pause*) your own (*pause*) your very own (*pause*) Bessie Bunter.'

'I can only make one conclusion (*pause*) utter catastrophe.'

'And finally (*pause*) I would like to say just this (*pause*). Goodbye and (*pause*) good luck.'

And lastly, don't try and talk through interruptions, applause or any outside noises such as jet planes or fire alarms. Pause, make a humorous aside if you want—and then continue.

Timing is an art. Successful live comedians such as Billy Connolly and Dave Allen have it. So do chat and game show hosts such as Bruce Forsyth who are highly skilled at playing their audience. See how they anticipate audience reaction through clever use of pauses and timing.

Another thing to keep in mind in delivery is the importance of rhythm. Remember in Chapter 5 we spoke about 'the rule of threes'? For some strange reason, phrases neatly packaged into three succinct points can sometimes get a big audience on its feet applauding wildly.

Remember this famous one?—'Government for the people, of the people, by the people.'

And finally, keep an eye on the time but don't look at your watch—the audience will interpret that as boredom. Make sure you can see a clock, or take off your watch and put it in front of you where you can see it.

Ums and ers

We all um and er much more than we think. When fluency fails us and we need to think, these noises come crawling out of our mouth.

Try and resist the temptation to open your mouth when you are asked a question you don't know the answer to. Train yourself to think silently. Greville Janner fines his pupils every time they utter an 'um' or an 'er'. Get a friend to cough everytime they hear you produce one. Tape record yourself.

Signposts

In Chapter 5 we looked at the importance of building in 'signposts' when you are writing a speech. Now it's time to put it to the test. The audience don't have a script in front of them, so they can't tell what point you are at. You will need to keep them posted as to where you are—at point one, two or three.

Use your fingers as pointers if the group is small. Use the flipchart to mark the boundaries of your presentation: when you finish a point, flip back a piece of paper revealing a blank square before going onto your next point. Repeat yourself and don't be afraid to use redundant language. Here are some examples.

'We've talked about A and B. Now I want to come into the third and final point, C.'

Keeping your audience alive

You know the signs. You can see the fidgeting and hear a slow murmur. One or two people are sitting back with their hands behind their heads. Someone yawns. You are losing your audience.

There are several ploys you can use here:

- Hasten to the end and finish promptly.

- Move towards the audience (easy in a small group) and look around at each of them.

- Shake them up with a rhetorical question such as: 'How many of you here would really like to be doing something new with your lives?'

- Use a visual aid. Turn a page on the flipchart.

- Do something dramatic like rip off a page of the flipchart, crumple it up and throw it on the floor.

- Invite some kind of response from the audience. Ask for a show of hands. Ask a direct question to one named person. (It is useful to have these questions prepared beforehand, even if they are only in your head. The mind has a tendency to go blank at times like these.)

- Ask the audience to do something. Get them into small groups to discuss a point.

- Change something. Move your position. Go on to another subject. Take a break.

- And finally, to establish real rapport with the audience you do need to *enjoy* talking to them.

HUMOUR AND WIT

It is very difficult to be witty before an audience until you have a certain degree of confidence of speaking in public. Again, don't even attempt to tell a joke if you are not a good joke teller.

However, if you *can* use humour well your audience will love you and you will be able to make any subject more interesting. Laughter makes the audience relax and more receptive to what you are saying. Subjects to avoid are mother-in-law jokes, anything to do with religion, Irish or other racialist jokes, and jokes directed at named people (a relative, friend or admirer might be in the audience).

Relatively safe subjects for humour include:

- British Rail or London Transport—reference to 'let the train take the strain' said tongue in cheek might cause a titter amongst weary commuters.
- Bureaucracy—tales of the inefficiency of faceless departments and officialese.
- 'That's life' consumer tales relating to British Gas, British Telecom or local cowboys.

Using the humour of everyday life is safer than trying to be too clever.

Keeping a cuttings file is a useful exercise. Books like *The Book of Heroic Failures* by Stephen Pile (Futura) could provide you with a fund of stories from life.

Here is just one. You could practise telling it aloud:

THE LEAST SUCCESSFUL WEATHER REPORT

After severe flooding in Jeddah, Saudi Arabia, in January 1979, the *Arab News* gave the following bulletin: 'We regret we are unable to give you the weather. We rely on weather reports from the airport, which is closed because of the weather. Whether we are able to give you the weather tomorrow will depend on the weather.'

Don't
- say you are going to tell a funny story;
- laugh at your own humour;
- try and be clever by using an accent unless you can really carry it off;
- pick on people in the audience;
- pick a sensitive subject;
- be apologetic.

DEALING WITH AUDIENCE FEEDBACK

Answering questions
You may need to decide beforehand whether to take questions during your presentation or to ask people to wait until the end. Sometimes impromptu questions during your speech can be highly constructive; they show you the audience is interested and you can use this to encourage participation. However, questions like this can be disruptive; it is easy to go off at a tangent and become involved in an irrelevant argument. Avoid being drawn in. Your answers should be concise and to the point.

Here are some points to bear in mind when answering questions.

- *The question you can't answer.*
  If you can't answer the question, say 'I'm sorry, I can't answer that one, but I can refer you to...' *Never* bluff your way out of it. Another way of dealing with a question you can't answer is to 'field it' back to the audience. 'That's a very interesting question. Would anyone in the audience like to make a comment?'

  There are ways of playing for time whilst you think. Try these. (1) Take a drink of water first. (2) Say 'That's a very interesting question. I'm glad you asked me that one. But before I answer it I would like to make just one point...' Politicians are

notorious for dodging tricky questions using this technique.
(3) Stop and think. Pause. It gives the impression of sincerity—
that your reply is coming from the heart.

- *The irrelevant question.*
  If the question is totally off the point and of no interest to
  anyone else, ask that person to see you afterwards, when you
  will deal with the question personally.

- *The personal attack.*
  This usually takes the form of a question like. 'Do you really
  think you are qualified to speak on this subject, Mr Block,
  when you have never experienced poverty?' This can throw
  some people. Having something up your sleeve for dealing with
  these kind of questions helps. Try statements like: 'I appreciate
  your question, Mr Heckler, but I *have* experienced poverty'; or
  'It is not necessary to experience something directly to be
  sympathetic towards it. You don't necessarily have to be a
  woman to understand how women think'.

- *The loaded question.*
  These usually include an assumption and then go on to ask a
  question. Watch out for questions like 'When did you last beat
  your wife?' and 'How long have you been cheating the
  taxpayer?' These examples are obvious, but they illustrate the
  point. Your reply should be in two stages. Firstly, refute the
  assumption that you have been beating your wife/cheating the
  taxpayer. Then go on to make the point you wanted.

- *The point of information.*
  Someone puts up their hand and says: 'Point of information.
  Your facts are incorrect!' and then proceeds to produce some
  new statistics. There may not be much you can do about that,
  except to thank them for their point and carry on.

Other hints for dealing with questions

- Don't get pompous and flaunt your knowledge.
- Listen carefully and ask the person to repeat the question if
  necessary. If you don't understand the question then ask for
  clarification.
- Never lie.
- Answer the question only. Don't start a new subject.

- If the questioner comes back with 'Yes but ...' and looks like starting a dialogue or argument, cut them short, politely, and go onto the next question.

- If the question turns out to be a statement, interrupt and ask the person what exactly the question is. If you don't want to encourage free debate you will have to do this.

- Watch out for people with their hands up who have not had a chance to put a question.

- Ask for the questioner's name before replying or ask all questioners to give their name first.

- If you invite questions from the audience and are met with a stony silence then ask *them* a question. You can always have a 'plant'—someone who is primed to ask a particular question.

Dealing with hecklers and interruptions

The secret is not to be thrown by interruptions or disturbances but to use them to your advantage. The Methodist leader the Rev Donald Soper used to appear regularly in London at Speakers' Corner and Tower Hill on his soap box preaching to crowds; he was a master at dealing with hecklers, using his sharp wit to raise a laugh.

Don't try and be clever unless it comes naturally to you—it will fall flat and make you look stupid. Deal with the problem firmly and assertively with comments like: 'Mr Heckler, I appreciate you have a point of view, but would you have the courtesy to wait until I have finished speaking, when I will be glad to answer your question.' You *must* be extremely positive without becoming angry. If the heckler continues you may need to get someone else to remove him (or her). Never try and talk through a heckler and don't get drawn into an argument. As a last resort you could offer the heckler the platform and let the audience deal with him by booing him off.

IMPROVISING

Take this situation. You are leaving your job to go to another one. It's the Christmas party. Suddenly, someone makes an announcement and proposes a toast. 'We are very sorry to be losing Jane, who has been with us for nearly five years now. I know that she would like to say a few words.' You feel a lurch in your stomach. This is totally unexpected. Whatever do you say?

You are sitting quietly in a committee meeting minding your own business. The chairman turns to you and says: 'Peter, what do *you* think?'

If you are really taken unawares and don't know what to say, then the best task is to be totally honest. Take the situation of having to make a speech at your leaving party. Something like this would suffice. 'You've caught me on the hop. I had planned on sliding quietly away. It seems that I'm not going to be allowed to do that. So all I would like to say is that I've really enjoyed working here and I'll miss you all.'

Like many things, being able to talk off the cuff is a matter of practice and confidence. Some people plan for these kind of situations and make it seem as if they are speaking off the top of their head. Some people have a handful of little anecdotes and quotations they bring out on occasions like this.

Some useful exercises found in public speaking courses are to pick a subject or a single word and try talking for one minute on that subject. It could be anything—parties, water sports, women MPs or more obscure things like coathangers, oranges and feet. Try it. You'll find that one minute can seem an awful long time.

BBC Question Time
Another useful discipline is to read the papers and imagine you are on BBC TV's *Question Time* and being asked direct questions about topical subjects. Here are two for practice.

Should a person who has had a sex change be allowed to marry under British law? (Assume they want to marry someone of the same sex as they started life as.)

'What do you think the Government should do to attract more science specialists into the teaching profession?'

Watch programmes like these and listen to radio phone-ins, too.

When you have been put on the spot
Take the situation of the committee meeting again. There are several ways out of the dilemma (especially if you have been half asleep):

- ask for more time to consider;
- say you need to bring the matter to the attention of your department/colleagues before making a statement, as you don't feel you can represent their views before consulting them;
- summarize what people have already said and say, 'Well, I agree with ...'

- reply by asking a question for clarification.

Some more techniques to get you out of a jam include:

- turning the subject around so that you make the point you want to anyway by dodging the question;
- having the outline of a speech ready just in case;
- getting someone to repeat the question to give you more time to think;
- making three simple points before you shut up.

AUDIENCE PARTICIPATION

Getting your audience to do some activities is a good way to get them involved and keep their attention. If you are running a workshop or training session then it is essential. There isn't space here to go into much detail, but here are some simple techniques for getting your audience involved.

- Divide them into small groups to brainstorm some thoughts on a given topic.
- Give them a problem or case study to solve.
- Ask them to turn and introduce themselves to their neighbour.
- Invite them to write three points they would like to deal with during the day.

If you haven't done this before, try it out on a friend or try it out yourself. If you find the exercises difficult or unclear then they will need revising.

An ice-breaker

Try this 'ice-breaker' exercise. Give a group a list of subjects such as (a) sign of the zodiac, (b) tennis, (c) only child, (d) living in Wales. Ask them to find someone in the group who shares the same sign of the zodiac, plays tennis, is an only child and lives in Wales (one person for each point). You will find your group suddenly comes alive and is much more receptive. This exercise works wonders.

It is important to establish rapport very quickly with an audience, especially if they are a small group or you are teaching them rather than speaking to them. Asking questions early on and getting them to *do* something will help to make contact. Use the word *YOU* and avoid the word *I*.

FINAL CHECKLIST ON THE DAY

Before you start

__ Check all equipment before you start to make sure it's working.

__ If you are using an overhead projector or slide projector check all parts of the room to make sure every member of your audience can see. (There will be some 'dead' space where part of the equipment blocks the screen.)

__ Are all your visual aids ready in the right order?

__ Are there enough sheets of paper on the flipchart?

__ Do you know where the light switches are? Can you dim them?

__ Can you see a watch or clock easily?

__ Is the room set out as you would like it? If people need to make notes do they need tables? Is the layout right for the style of presentation?

__ Have you checked that the audience is who you think they are? If there is a delegate list or class list look it through; take note of names and where they are from.

__ Have you checked for risqué jokes and sensitive subjects?

__ Feeling nervous? Ready to try some deep breathing to calm yourself down?

__ Don't eat or drink any of the following: alcohol, fizzy drinks (you might burp), or heavy food.

__ Ask yourself, 'What single point I am trying to get across to the audience?' and 'What change would I like them to experience in themselves?'

__ Remember AIDA—Attention, Interest, Desire, Action.

__ Walk confidently into the room. Stand and look at the audience. Pause. If you are being introduced, wait—and then begin.

During your speech

- Start with a shocking statement that will make them sit up and listen. Try something like this for a talk on health. 'There are a hundred of you in this room. 43 of you will die of a heart attack, 4 will be the victims of road accidents, 39 will die of cancer, 3 of excess of alcohol and one of AIDS—statistically, that is.'

- Remember to avoid the ostrich position—don't bury your head in the script. Make sure you look at the audience.

- Don't forget to pause.

- Imagine the audience as a bunch of your best friends.

- Leave your hands free for gestures. Remember to make large gestures—half-hearted ones look silly. Gestures should relate to what you are saying. Don't talk about expansion whilst holding your hands six inches apart.

- If your voice starts to get shaky or you dry up then stop for a moment, look at your script, take a deep breath—and carry on. Whilst the time may seem like an age to you, the audience won't perceive it as so long.

- If your voice gets a bit croaky or you start to lose it then pause for a moment, cough if you need to or have a drink of water, clear your throat and continue.

- Deal with interruptions by pausing and politely asking the person to make their comments when you have finished.

After your presentation

- Remember to deal with questions honestly. Never waffle if you don't know the answer.

- Say 'thank you' to the audience for listening.

- Never end with 'Well that's about it then' or in some other half-hearted way. End with something positive and noteworthy.

Some tips from the top

Finally, here are some comments by well-known speakers taken from *The Secrets of Successful Speaking* by Gordon Bell.

'Make sure you know your subject well; leave nothing to chance and then you can leave everything to chance... If you know your subject it will come over easily and naturally.' (Viscount Tonypandy, former Speaker of the House of Commons).

'Be yourself. Know your subject. Talk—don't read.' (Baroness Phillips).

'Don't rehearse too meticulously. Don't learn things by heart—and certainly not other people's poetry... Don't go on too long. If the public is wonderful, stop a little short of total triumph.' (Peter Ustinov).

'Always prepare even if you think you might not be called upon to speak.' (Rachel Heyhoe Flint).

11
Dealing with the Media

The rules of public speaking take on a new guise when the electronic media of radio and television are involved. The appearance of a camera or microphone can do strange things to the voice and face: the camera 'loves' some people more than others. Since the 1960s, politicians have stood or fallen by their success on radio and television, particularly on the latter. We have seen the demise of highly competent and articulate politicians like former Prime Minster Sir Alec Douglas Home, and the rise of media men like Ronald Reagan, all because of how their face fitted on the small screen. Lloyd George was a brilliant Parliamentary orator but he didn't succeed on radio because he addressed the microphone as if it were a public meeting; for the medium of radio a much more intimate style was needed.

So in what circumstances might *you* find yourself appearing on radio or television and having to deal with the broadcasting media? You might be asked to speak on behalf of your Trade Union or Professional Association, a voluntary organisation, college or university or you simply have a story to tell and something to say. You might find yourself in the audience of *Question Time* or *Kilroy*, or be interviewed for a documentary radio or TV programme.

So what is the difference between speaking to a live audience in a hall and talking to a mass audience you can't see via the electronic media?

Firstly, you will probably be interviewed by a broadcasting professional; he or she will be a much better communicator than you are and very adept at asking tricky questions. If you are lucky you will get an interviewer who helps you and goes out of their way to make you feel relaxed. If you are unlucky you will get an aggressive Robin Day or Brian Walden type.

Secondly, the presence of a microphone or TV camera tends to make people stiffen up or gives them fits of the giggles. They can find it very difficult to be natural. Actors and politicians are generally used to the cameras; industrialists, business people, members of the police and armed forces are not. People in these latter groups often look and sound excruciatingly boring and fail to put their point across.

Thirdly, radio and TV is a much more intimate medium. You don't need to raise your voice or use expansive gestures. The technique is much more like the fireside chat.

Fourthly, you have much less time to put across your point and therefore need to be brief. The buzz word here is 'sound bites'—catch phrases of 5 to 10 words. Journalists love neat little quotes of one sentence like 'The lady's not for turning' because they linger in the public's memory and are eminently quotable.

Golden rules for anyone being interviewed on radio and TV
Although there are differences in style between radio and TV there are some general rules that apply to both:

- Arrive on time for your interview. Studio time is at a premium.

- Try to have three main points ready and get them across no matter what. You don't have to answer the questions directly—most politicians dodge them when it suits them.

- Take cards with statistics and specific information with you if necessary for reference. (This is easier on radio than TV.)

- Don't be led off at a tangent during questioning. If the interview is all about teachers' pay and the questioner starts asking you about fees for marking examination papers or classroom appraisal, politely point out that the interview is about teachers' pay and return to the point.

- Similarly don't fall into the trap of answering a loaded question like: 'How long had you been plotting to overthrow the Prime Minster?' A good answer would simply be: 'I have never been involved in any plot to overthrow the Prime Minister.'

- 'No comment' as a reply to a leading question might do if you happen to be having a romance with a member of the Royal Family. However, if you are representing a large company which has just been accused of polluting the rivers, 'no comment' is tantamount to admitting guilt—and it looks as if you don't care.

- If you don't know the answer, simply say that you can't answer that question at the moment.

- It's a good idea to discuss the content of the interview beforehand so that you don't get caught with a question you hadn't prepared for. However, your interviewer may not respect your wishes and may still spring an awkward question on you. Don't feel pressured into replying—you can say that you didn't agree to talk about x.

- Don't ramble. Make your point clearly and firmly, then shut up.

- Be positive. 'That is totally untrue' will impress the audience much more than 'We-ll, not really.'

- Don't get drawn into an argument. Make your point clearly and don't be bullied. Above all, *never* lose your temper and fling the microphone on the floor (as some politicians have done). Keep your cool and reiterate your point.

- Don't use professional jargon unless it is widely understood. Most people know that TUC stands for the Trades Union Congress, but few people know that NATFHE stands for the National Association of Teachers in Further and Higher Education.

- Try and avoid 'ums' and 'ers', especially on television as they cannot be edited out.

- Don't drink too much alcohol before an interview.

- Don't use swear words. Even 'bloody' may offend.

- Try and tell good news.

- Never patronise your audience.

- A WORD OF WARNING. *Never* say anything 'off the record' when you are in a studio. Too many people have fallen into the trap of assuming that the tape is no longer running when the interview is over. The really cunning interviewer may try this one on you: 'Well, now that the interview is over, tell me what you *really* think.' The interviewee is duped into saying something really damaging which is then recorded on tape and used out of context.

   The other catch is during the 'warm up' when the producer will ask you for a few words for **level**. Greville Janner tells a story about Ronald Reagan just before a crucial radio broadcast when he was asked to say a few words about the United States Economy for 'sound levels'. 'I must tell the nation,' said the

President, 'that our economy is in one hell of a mess!' Unfortunately, the studio was already linked up to loudspeakers in the White House and Press Room and his words were heard loud and clear all around the world!

Special considerations: radio

One advantage of radio is that you don't have to worry about what you look like, whether your nose is shining and whether you are wearing the right colours. It's much less threatening. However, if you happen to have a tinny voice then people will assume that you are a tinny person because they can't see you. The other danger is to relax *too* much and be led into saying things you didn't really mean.

On radio it is easier to edit tape without it appearing disjointed, because there's no worry about picture continuity. All your 'ums' and 'ahs' can miraculously disappear, making you sound wonderfully fluent. The disadvantage is that it is much easier to move phrases around and distort the meaning because it is less easy to detect in sound.

Other tips for radio:
- Don't wear jangly jewellery or tap the table with your fingers.
- Treat the interviewer like a friend you're having a chat with. You don't have to lecture them or declaim loudly.
- If you make a mess of your reply (assuming the interview is pre-recorded) then stop and ask if you can start again.
- If your voice gets croaky, sip a glass of water.

Special considerations: television

Television adds complications because you can see as well as hear. Large noses for example appear even larger and overhanging stomachs look huge. But the camera can also hide a few wrinkles. People take more notice of what they see than what they hear. So if you want to be taken seriously you must look sincere and credible.

Here are some special tips for dealing with television.

- Look at your interviewer and don't avert your gaze. Unfortunately, on television, people who move their eyes around looking up, down and sideways end up looking shifty and indecisive. Avoid glancing up at the clock or the audience in case the camera catches you. If you're asked a difficult question, try not to search the air for answers.

- When making your main points, look straight at the interviewer. Sound authoritative and emphatic, state your three main points clearly—then sit back and stop,.

- Keep gestures to the minimum. They don't look good on television as a rule.

- Try not to fiddle with your hair or hands. Some cameramen are apt to focus on people playing with their hands. If you want to know if the camera is on you, look for the red light.

- A glass of water will help if you need time to think.

- Don't slouch—it makes you look sloppy. On the other hand don't sit too upright—it makes you look nervous and inflexible. Try and find a relaxed asymmetrical way of sitting.

- If you are reading a script try not to look up and down. Eyes moving up and down will make you look guilty and people may not believe what you say.

- Autocue and Portaprompt (the device which runs the script on a scroll through a camera at eye level) help keep the presenter's eye in line with the camera. Reading Autocue is a knack, but not too difficult if you read well. (See Chapter 6 for the section on 'How to make a text sound said, not read'.)

- Avoid the following clothes:
  Black and white.
  Checks, narrow stripes and shiny clothes—they tend to create a 'strobe' effect on screen.
  Complicated patterns.
  Fussy, frilly accessories and trimmings.
  Scruffy clothes—they will look even worse on TV.
  Flashy jewellery.
  Clothes than tend to 'ride up' when you sit down. Sit on the bottom of your jacket to pull it well down.

- Watch the interviewer for cues. When they want you to speak they will give you all kinds of verbal signals indicating that it's your turn—change of posture, sitting back instead of forward.

- If you're in a group situation as in BBC's *Question Time* don't lose concentration when others are speaking. If they say something you don't agree with, shake your head—the camera will pick it up as a **reaction shot**; you will have made your point without uttering a single word.

- Make sure you get the last word and keep it short. Prepare one final sentence to hit them with at the end, say it, then sit back and shut up.

- Remember to smile, look enthusiastic and enjoy yourself. And above all, be yourself.

There are plenty of courses in how to appear on radio and television. They can be rather expensive but could be essential for anyone acting as a spokesperson for an organisation.

Answers to exercises on page 129

1 Any of the following:
   Diagram reproduced onto OHP transparency.
   Diagram drawn onto flipchart or large sheet of paper on wall.
   Diagram on handout (not as good as the above).

2 Handout with details of figures.

3 Flipchart to record points made by trainees.
   Key points on prepared sheets.
   Video—preferably humorous.

4 Video showing animatic of proposed campaign.
   Storyboard on large card.
   Visuals on large card.
   Slides.

5 The actual piece of equipment.
   Handout material with step-by-step instructions.
   Possible explanatory video.
   (You may need to split the group into smaller groups).

6 Objects (antiques).
   Slides.

7 Flipchart
   Handout (to give out after speaking.)

8 Slides.
   OHP (only if the lettering is large enough).

9 The product.
   Press pack with information and photography.
   Slides showing product(s) and possibly its production.
   Video showing product in use.

Glossary

Acronym A word formed from initial letters of other words. Example: NALGO (National Association of Local Government Officers).

Alexander Technique Technique and series of exercises intended to realign the posture and relax the muscles, encouraging better vocal quality and general well-being.

Audience The receiver(s) of a communication message, generally the people to whom a speaker is addressing their presentation. Understanding the needs of the audience is crucial to successful public speaking.

Autocue A device which enables a speaker or presenter to read whilst looking directly at the audience. On television, a narrow strip of paper is fed through a screen directly in the eye line of the presenter (usually just under or in the camera). At conferences, the text is projected on to a clear glass screen in front of the lectern whilst the scroll is fed through a machine behind-the-scenes at the appropriate speed.

Body language The overt and covert (hidden) messages which are communicated through posture, gestures, bodily movement, facial expression and so on. All bodily communication is non verbal. Example: Slouched posture can convey boredom, poor self image, or disgust.

Brainstorming A procedure for generating ideas in which participants use word association. The idea is not to comment on suggestions or make any criticism but to let the imagination flow. The technique can also be practised by an individual.

Channel The medium used for communicating a message – the telephone line, the newspaper, a letter or television, for instance. The communication 'channel' is a line along which communication passes. So *speech* is not a channel – but soundwaves through air *is* a channel.

Cliché A well worn phrase or expression which has lost its originality and appeal. Example: There's no smoke without fire. To be avoided in a speech, if possible.

Code The 'language' in which a message is sent eg: speech, Morse code, semaphore, writing. The word 'code' suggests that the language had to be learned as if it were a strange language like Chinese.

Communication models Theories or structures (often represented by diagrams) which attempt to explain or put into some framework, the process of communication.

Decoder The person(s) or thing which translates the code into something meaningful, such as an interpreter or an unscrambling device. Even when you are listening or reading in your native language, your brain still acts as a decoder for sounds and visual symbols.

Encoder The person(s) or thing which translates the message into code. When you turn your ideas into speech or writing you are encoding.

Eye contact The degree of gaze a person maintains with another person. Eye contact with an audience is crucial in all presentations as it opens up and maintains the 'visual channel'.

Hidden agenda The ulterior motives or undisclosed reasons behind overt (stated) behaviour. Every meeting has a declared agenda or items to be discussed, and a number of personal items particular to each individual (hidden agenda).

Intonation The degree to which the voice rises and falls in normal conversation. Intonation is determined by the stress put on each word or part of a sentence. Differing intonation can alter the meaning of the same sentence significantly.

Inversion Turning the normal order of words in a sentence upside-down. Example: 'Ask not what your country can do for you. Ask what you can do for your country.'

Jargon Specialized language generally only understood by particular groups such as professions. Jargon is to be avoided unless the speaker is sure all members of the audience are familiar with the words.

Key words The most important words in a speech which are written onto cue cards (or a flip chart) to aid recall or summarise the main points.

Language A code which normally uses words, but can also use visual signals or non-verbal sounds (as in 'body language' or 'the language of music'). The code (eg words) are arranged in some order (eg a sentence) according to certain rules of grammar (syntax).

Law of primacy The tendency for people to remember the first things heard or seen.

The law of recency The tendency for people to remember the last things heard or seen.

Learning or concentration curve The degree to which people absorb new information or skills during a defined period. Normally, people absorb more at the beginning, then the 'curve' dips steeply and only rises towards the end of the period. (See *Law of primacy* and *Law of recency*).

Media Literally, the plural of 'medium'. In this context it refers to the 'mass media' of communication—radio, television, the press, etc.

Message The content of a communication—*what* is being communicated.

Metaphor The application of an imaginary or figurative characteristic to an object or person. Metaphors often imbue things with human characteristics—and vice-versa. Examples: Food for thought. The waves roared.

Mind mapping The process of taking random ideas and putting them down on paper in a random manner (not in the form of a list) like a map.

Motivation The reason(s) behind human behaviour. What drives people along certain paths of action.

Noise Literally, a loud unpleasant sound. In the context of communication theory it refers to anything which interferes with the process of communication eg: crackling on a microphone, muffled speech, poor vision, illegible writing.

Non-verbal communication Communication without words. Includes body language, facial expressions, clothes, pictures, visual symbols and music.

Objectives Specific goals or outcomes which can be measured or quantified.

Oratory The art of charismatic public speaking.

Orientation Where people and things are in relation to each other. Refers to distance and angle (above, below, to one side, etc.)

Overhead projector Piece of equipment for projecting material written or printed on transparencies. (Not to be confused with a slide projector where photographs on 35mm transparencies are projected onto a screen).

Parallelism Two statements which are similar. Example: 'I sighed as a lover, I obeyed as a son'. (Gibbon).

Projection The ability to 'throw' the voice over distances.

Receiver The person or audience to which the communicator (sender) is addressing the message.

Redundancy Language or words which are not absolutely necessary for communication of the message. Often referred to as 'padding'. Redundant language is important in *oral* communication because it reinforces the message and adds rhythm.

Rhetoric The art of persuasive and eloquent speech or writing.

Rhetorical question A question which needs no answer, as it is designed just for dramatic effect.

Sender Person or thing who is initiating the communication to the audience (receiver).

Signposts Verbal markers in a speech which give the audience clues as to where they are. Examples 'firstly', 'next' and 'finally'.

Simile A figure of speech in which one thing (or person) is compared to another. Example: As alike as two peas in a pod).

Sources – primary Information or data gained directly from people.

Sources – secondary Information or data gained from books, reports, newspapers, mainly indirect written forms of communication.

Syntax The rules of grammar and sentence construction.

Tone The sound the voice makes—soft, harsh, strident, shrill, gruff, mellow, resonant, etc.

Verbiage Needlessly wordy language.

Further Reading

Dictionaries and books of quotations
The Concise Oxford Dictionary of Quotations.
The Penguin Dictionary of Modern Quotations.
The Pan/Chambers Book of Business Quotations.
Guide to Political Quotations (Longman pocket companion series).
Contradictory quotations, Colin Bowles (Angus & Robertson).

Facts, trivia, jokes and stories
The Best of British Trivia, Jim and Penny Converse (Javelin).
The 637 Best Things Anybody Ever Said, Robert Byrne (Sphere).
100% British, Jo Eastwood (Penguin).
Not Many People Know That, Michael Caine.
The Book of Journologists (The Mail on Sunday's YOU magazine).
Jokes, Quotes and One-Liners for Public Speakers, Henry V. Prochnow
    and Herbert V. Prochnow Junior (Thorsons).
The Book of Heroic Failures, Stephen Pile (Futura).
The Return of Heroic Failures (Penguin).

Books on public speaking
Put it together, Put it across, David Bernstein (Cassell).
How to Give a Successful Presentation, Ian Richards.
Present Yourself, Michael Gelb (Aurium).
The secrets of successful speaking and business presentations,
    Gordon Bell.
Effective Speaking, Christina Stuart (Pan).
Janner's complete speechmaker, Greville Janner (Business Books).
Readymade speeches, Barry Turner (Kogan Page).
How to Make a Wedding Speech, John Bowden (How To Books).
Sample Social Speeches, Gordon Williams (Paper Front).
The Bluffer's Guide to Public Speaking, Chris Steward and Mike
    Wilkinson (Ravetto).

Miscellaneous reading
Put it in Writing, John Whale (Dent).
The Complete Plain Words, Sir Ernest Gowers (Pelican).
The Book of Similes, Robert Baldwin and Ruth Paris (Futura).
Body Language, Michael Pease (Positive Paperbacks).
Use Your Head, Tony Buzan (BBC/Open University).
How to Communicate at Work, Ann Dobson (How To Books)

Index